SKILL PRACTICE

GRADE 1

IncentivePublications
BY WORLD BOOK

Many thanks to Charlotte Poulos and Laurie Grupé,
whose adapted exercises are included in this book.

Written by Imogene Forte and Marjorie Frank
Illustrated by Kathleen Bullock
Cover by Brenda Tropinski

Print Edition ISBN 978-1-62950-480-3
E-book Edition ISBN 978-1-62950-481-0 (PDF)

World Book, Inc.
180 North LaSalle Street
Suite 900
Chicago, Illinois 60601
USA

For information about World Book and Incentive Publications products, call **1-800-967-5325,** or visit our websites at **www.worldbook.com** and **www.incentivepublications.com.**

Printed in the United States of America by Sheridan Books, Inc.
Chelsea, Michigan
1st printing June 2016

TABLE OF CONTENTS

Language, Writing, & Usage Exercises

Social Studies

Social Studies Exercises

Map Skills & Geography Exercises

Science 187

Science Exercises

Math 227

Math Computation & Problem Solving Exercises

INTRODUCTION

Do basic skills have to be boring? Absolutely not! Mastery of basic skills provides the foundation for exciting learning opportunities for students. Content relevant to their everyday life is fascinating stuff! Kids love learning about topics such as galaxies and glaciers, thunderstorms and timelines, continents and chemicals, tarantulas and tornadoes, poems and plateaus, elephants and encyclopedias, mixtures and mummies, antonyms and Antarctica, and more. Using these topics and carefully designed practice they develop basic skills that ponder, process, grow, and achieve school success.

Acquiring, polishing, and using basic skills and content is a cause for celebration—not an exercise in drudgery. *Skill Practice: Grade 1* invites students to sharpen their abilities in the essentials of language arts, social studies, science, and mathematics.

As you examine *Skill Practice: Grade 1,* you will see that it is filled with attractive, age-appropriate student exercises. These pages are no ordinary worksheets! *Skill Practice: Grade 1* contains hundreds of inventive and inviting ready-to-use lessons based on a captivating theme that invites the student to join an adventure, solve a puzzle, pursue a mystery, or tackle a problem. Additionally, each illustrated exercise provides diverse tools for reinforcement and extension of basic and higher-order thinking skills.

Skill Practice: Grade 1 contains the following components:

- A clear, sequential list of skills for eight different content areas. Checklists of skills begin each content section. These lists correlate with the exercises, identifying page numbers where specific skills can be practiced. Students can chart their progress by checking off each skill as it is mastered.

- **Over 300 pages of student exercises**
  Each exercise page:
  . . . addresses a specific basic skill or content area.
  . . . presents tasks that grab the attention and curiosity of students.
  . . . contains clear directions to the student.
  . . . asks students to use, remember, and practice a basic skill.
  . . . challenges students to think creatively and analytically.
  . . . requires students to apply the skill to real situations or content.
  . . . takes students on learning adventures with a variety of delightful characters!

- **A ready-to-use assessment tool**
  Four skills tests follow the skills exercises. The tests are presented in parts corresponding to the skills lists. Designed to be used as pre- or post-tests, individual parts of these tests can be given to students at separate times, if needed.

- **Complete answer keys**
  Easy-to-find-and-use answer keys for all exercises and skills tests follow each section.

HOW TO USE THIS BOOK:

The exercises contained in *Skill Practice: Grade 1* are to be used with adult assistance. The adult may serve as a guide to ensure the student understands the directions and questions.

Skill Practice: Grade 1 is designed to be used in many diverse ways. Its use will vary according to the needs of the students and the structure of the learning environment.

The skills checklists may be used as:
. . . record-keeping tools to track individual skills mastery;
. . . planning guides for instruction; and
. . . a place for students to proudly check off accomplishments.

Each exercise page may be used as:
. . . a pre-test or check to see how well a student has mastered a skill;
. . . one of many resources or exercises for teaching a skill;
. . . a way to practice or polish a skill that has been taught;
. . . a review of a skill taught earlier;
. . . reinforcement of a single basic skill, skills cluster, or content base;
. . . a preview to help identify instructional needs; and
. . . an assessment for a skill that a student has practiced.

The exercises are flexibly designed for presentation in many formats and settings. They are useful for individual instruction or independent work. They can also be used under the direction of an adult with small groups.

The skills tests may be used as:
. . . pre-tests to gauge instructional or placement needs;
. . . information sources to help adjust instruction; and
. . . post-tests to review student mastery of skills and content areas.

Skill Practice: Grade 1 is not intended to be a complete curriculum or textbook. It is a collection of inventive exercises to sharpen skills and provide students and parents with tools for reinforcing concepts and skills, and for identifying areas that need additional attention. This book offers a delightful assortment of tasks that give students just the practice they need—and to get that practice in a manner that is not boring.

As students take on the challenges of the enticing adventures in this book, they will increase their comfort level with the use of fundamental reading, writing, and language skills and concepts. Watching your student check off the sharpened skills is cause for celebration!

LANGUAGE ARTS

Skills Exercises
Grade One

Reading Spelling Vocabulary Grammar Writing

SKILLS CHECKLIST
PHONICS & WORD RECOGNITION

✔	SKILL	PAGE(S)
	Match uppercase to lowercase letters	21
	Recognize and discriminate between all letters of the alphabet	21, 22
	Put words in alphabetical order	22–23
	Identify and read beginning consonants	22–24, 27
	Recognize common sight words	23–24
	Use phonics to read whole words	23, 24, 44–51
	Distinguish between consonants and vowels	21, 22, 25, 26
	Identify and read beginning consonant blends	28, 29, 31
	Identify and read beginning consonant clusters & digraphs	28, 31
	Identify and read medial consonants	30
	Identify and read final consonants	32
	Identify and read words with double consonants	33
	Identify and read final consonant blends and digraphs	34
	Identify and read short vowels	35, 36
	Identify and read long vowels in words ending with silent *e*	37
	Identify and read long vowel sounds (vowel combinations)	38, 40, 42
	Identify and read diphthongs (*ow, ou*)	39
	Identify and read double vowel combinations (*oo, ee*)	41
	Recognize final *y* used as a vowel	43
	Identify and discriminate between synonyms & antonyms	44
	Identify and discriminate between homonyms	45
	Identify nouns	46
	Identify and read proper nouns	47
	Identify and read plural nouns	48
	Identify and read contractions	49
	Identify, read, and use rhyming words	50
	Identify and read compound words	51

SKILLS CHECKLIST
READING

✔	SKILL	PAGE(S)
	Read titles and match them to pictures	52, 53
	Create illustrations for sentences or passages	52, 63, 68
	Choose a good title for a passage	53, 70
	Read captions and match them to pictures	54
	Read sentences and match them to pictures	55
	Find information in illustrations	56, 57
	Find information on posters, maps, and graphs	58–60
	Identify the sequence of events in a passage	61–63
	Put words and sentences in proper sequence	61–63
	Follow written directions	64–65
	Locate facts or details in a passage	66–67
	Answer questions after reading a passage	66–67
	Make inferences about a passage	69
	Give a personal response to a passage	70
	Distinguish between homonyms	71
	Recognize high-frequency words	73
	Determine word meanings	72–77
	Recognize antonyms	72, 75
	Recognize synonyms	73, 75
	Classify words	74
	Use context to decide word meaning	76–77
	Choose the correct word for meaning in a sentence	76–77

SKILLS CHECKLIST
LANGUAGE, WRITING, & USAGE

✔	SKILL	PAGE(S)
	Write a short letter	78
	Express original ideas clearly in writing	78–87, 125
	Generate and organize ideas for writing	78–87, 1253
	Write clear, complete sentences	78, 80, 84, 85, 125
	Write a short paragraph	78, 80, 125
	Write phrases for a poster	79
	Write a short imaginative piece	80, 125
	Write similes	81
	Create good titles for written selections	82, 83
	Write descriptive words and phrases	86, 87
	Put words in alphabetical order	88
	Find correctly spelled words in a puzzle	89
	Identify, capitalize, and punctuate questions	90, 91, 94, 105, 117
	Identify, capitalize, and punctuate statements	90, 91, 95, 97, 98, 105, 113–116, 118
	Distinguish among statements, questions, & exclamations	90, 91, 105
	Identify, capitalize, and punctuate exclamations	90–92, 105, 106
	Identify and correct punctuation errors	90–96
	Identify different punctuation marks and their uses	90–96
	Place commas correctly in lists	93
	Correct words with incorrect capitalization	97
	Capitalize words in sentences	97–99, 113, 115
	Identify, write, and capitalize proper nouns	99, 97, 111
	Capitalize words in addresses	100
	Identify common contractions and words that form them	101
	Identify naming parts and action parts in sentences	102–104
	Identify and write verbs	107, 110, 119
	Identify and write nouns	107, 111, 112, 120–124
	Add *er* and *est* to adjectives to compare words	108
	Identify and write adjectives (describing words)	108-109
	Recognize and correct run-on sentences	113
	Distinguish among complete and incomplete sentences	113–116
	Identify complete sentences	113–116
	Identify and write possessive nouns	120
	Identify and write plural nouns	121, 123

Silly Soup

Bernie Bear is about to eat a bowl of letters.

What a funny kind of soup!

Draw a line to match each capital letter with its lowercase letter.

Circle the capital letters that are vowels.

Color the picture.

Name Aaratrika Paul

Upper- & Lowercase • Vowels

The Amazing ABC Mole Maze

Max and Matt are exploring a new tunnel.

Color the path in ABC order to help them find their way to a big surprise! Circle the letters that are consonants.

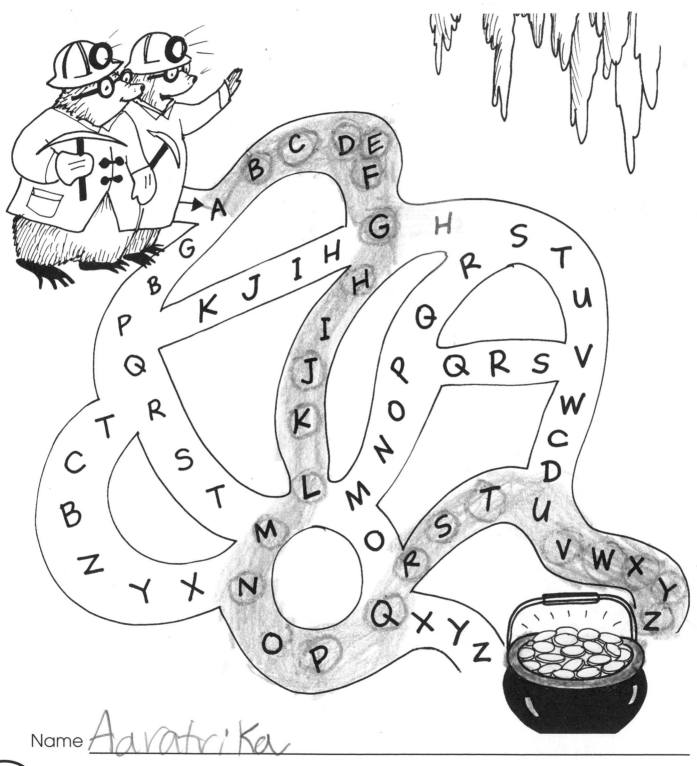

Name Aavatrika

ABC Order • Letter Discrimination • Consonants

An ABC Adventure

Molly Mouse is having a great adventure. Connect the dots in ABC order to find out what Molly is doing.

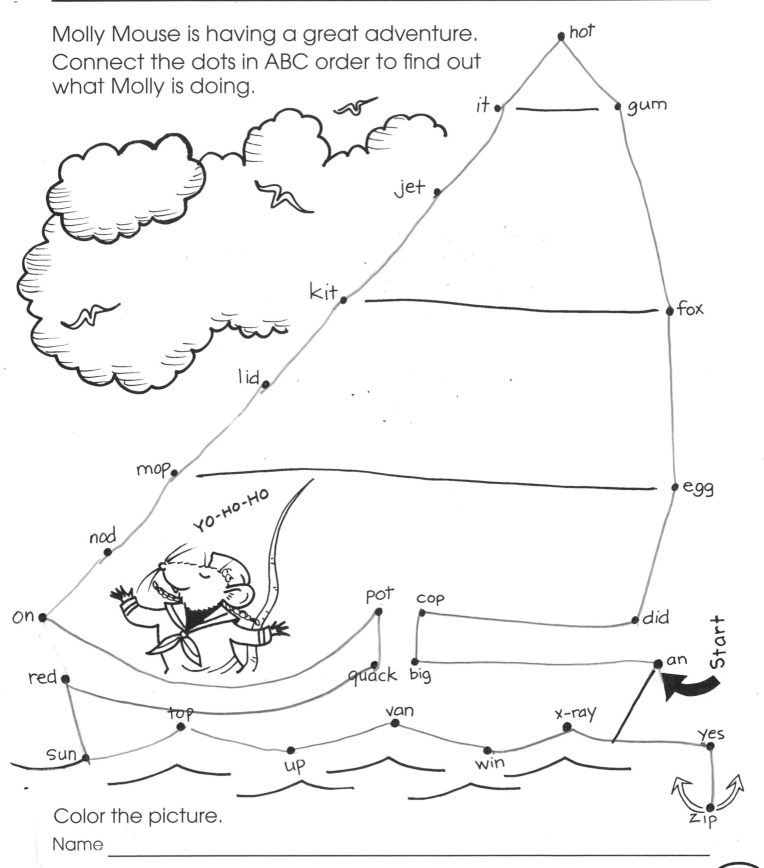

Color the picture.

Name _____

Ski Trouble

Oops! Poor Stella Squirrel has lost her ski.

Help her find it by coloring only the boxes that contain real words.

When you are finished, Stella will see a path to her lost ski.

stop	map	shut	twig
rif	mofe	ses	ten
sarn	twim	rope	sred
koj	make	pute	gik
shaz	fire	sees	star

Name _____

Sight Words

Underground Dinner

Misty Mole is ready for dinner.

To help her find the vegetables in her garden, color only the spaces that have consonants.

Do not color the spaces that have vowels.

Name _____

Distinguish Consonants & Vowels

Make a Quilt

Vowels are A, E, I, O, U. Consonants are all the other letters.

You can help Deb and Darla make a beautiful quilt.

Use your **blue** crayon to color each space that has a **vowel.**

Use your **red** crayon to color each space that has a **consonant.**

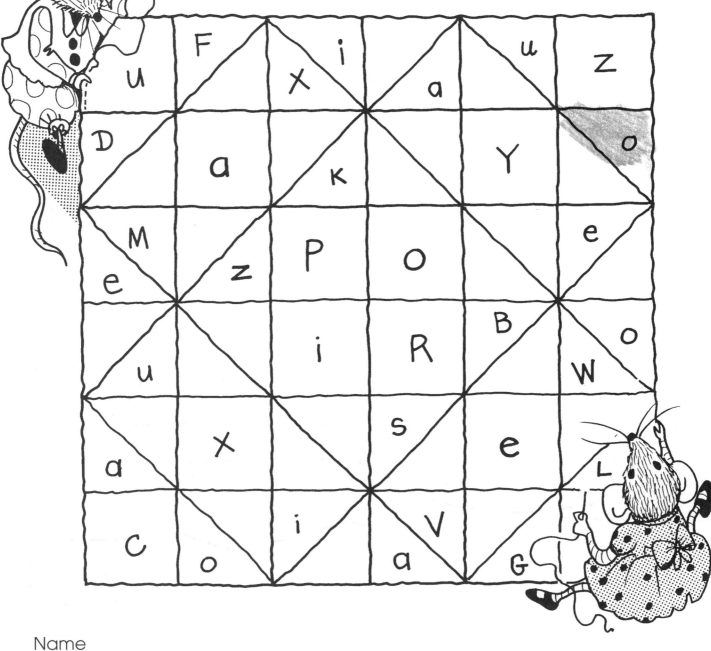

Name _____

Distinguish Consonants & Vowels

Hello! Hello!

Some furry friends are talking.

Each animal is saying the names of things that begin like his own name.

Find 3 things in the picture that begin with the same sound as **bear** and **bunny.**

     Color them **brown.**

Find 3 things that begin with the same sound as **fox.**

     Color them **orange.**

Find 3 things that begin with the same sound as **squirrel.**

     Color them **blue.**

Name _____

Beginning Consonants

Tricky Tongue Twisters

Busy Billy Blackbird is making tricky tongue twisters. You can, too! In each group of word pairs, circle the words that begin with the same sound.

To make funny tongue twisters, write the words you circled together on a line.

Write the words from the clouds on line 1.

Write the words from the kites on line 2.

Write the words from the flying disks on line 3.

1.
think
time

tub
thick

tree
thumbs

2.
witch
white

whale
west

watch
wheels

wrong
whistle

3.
chocolate
club

chair
cake

clock
chip

chain
croak

1. _____

2. _____

3. _____

Can you draw pictures of your silly sentences?

Name _____

Beginning Digraphs (th, wh, ch)

Hopping Frogs

Trace the letters that are consonant blends.
Then read the story to find out how to color the picture.
Circle the color word that makes the story silly.

Happy green frogs hop over

a blue creek.

Bright red flowers peek up

from the brown ground.

Gray clouds blow blue rain

down on the pink grass.

Name _____

Beginning Consonant Blends (br, cr, fr, gr, bl, cl)

A Day in the Desert

What things share the desert home with Louie Lizard?
Look at the name under each picture.
Find the missing letter in the box.
Write the missing letter in the middle of each word.

1. de_ert

4. ti_i

5. flo_er

p n s d b w z

2. po_y

6. ti_ard

3. sha_ow

7. ro_in

Color the pictures.

Name _____

Medial Consonants

Snow School

Pipi and Pete Penguin go to snow school.
Help them read some words they are
learning at school.

Use the words in the **Word Box** to
label each picture.

2. _____

1. school

3. _____

Word Box

school
snowman
sled
square
skates
scarf

4. _____

5. _____   6. _____

Color the picture.

Name _____

Beginning Blends & Clusters (sc, sk, sl, sn, squ, sch)

Tic-Tac-Toe

Tommy Tiger loves to play Tic-Tac-Toe.
Play some games with Tommy.
Look at each game.
Draw a line to connect 3 things
that have the same ending sound.

Final Consonants

Riddle-Dee-Dee

Olly and Dolly Owl are trying to solve some riddles.

Help them choose a word from the **Word Box** that will answer each riddle.

All the words have double letters.

Write each answer on the line.

Circle the double letters in your answer.

Then draw and color a picture of each answer.

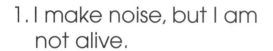

1. I make noise, but I am not alive.

   Babies like to play with me.

   I am a _____.

3. I grow on trees.

   I am good to eat.

   I am nature's toothbrush.

   I am an _____.

2. I am soft.

   I hop.

   I have long ears.

   I am a _____.

4. I appear after a rain.

   Kids love to play with me.

   I splash on their feet.

   I am a _____.

Word Box

rattle   bunny   puddle   apple

Name _____

Double Consonants

Ellie Is a Puzzle

No one knows much about Ellie.

Ellie is like a big secret.

Read each word scattered on the page.

Then write the words in their correct spaces in the puzzle.

The word that appears in the boxes will tell you who Ellie really is!

Trace Ellie's picture with a purple crayon.

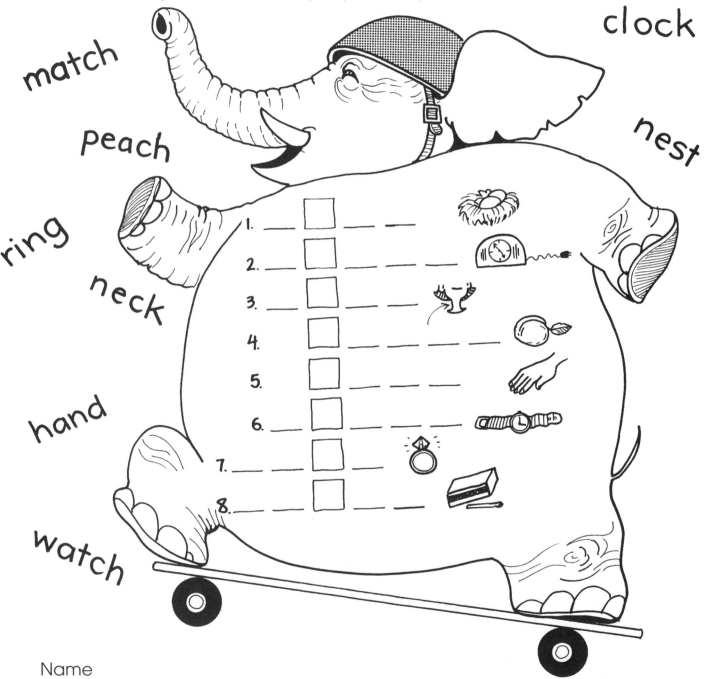

match

clock

Peach

nest

ring

neck

hand

watch

1.

2.

3.

4.

5.

6.

7.

8.

Name _____

Final Blends & Digraphs (ch, ck, nd, ng, st)

Bird Watcher

Kitty is a bird watcher.

Today she has found no birds.

She has spotted some funny things.

Look for 10 hidden pictures.

Color hidden things that have a **short i** sound (like pig) red.

Color hidden things that have a **short u** sound (like mud) green.

Name _____

Short Vowels (*i* and *u*)

Off to Africa!

Anna Banana and Robbie Bobba are going on a safari.
Help them pack.
In Anna's trunk, draw the things with a **short a** sound (like hat).
In Robbie's trunk, draw the things with a **short o** sound (like hot).

Color the pictures.

Name _____

Short Vowels (a and o)

Words Take a Ride

Five **silent e** words are riding the roller coaster.

What a silly thing for words to do!

Can you add letters to find the word in each car?

Use the words hidden in the **Word Puzzle.**

Color the words you find in the **Word Puzzle.**

Word Puzzle

F	C	A	K	E
I	Z	B	I	F
R	S	I	T	A
E	P	K	E	C
X	W	E	Q	E

Name _____

Silent e

Yummm-Yum!

Look at all the good things in the picnic basket.
Which foods have names with a long vowel sound?
Color everything in the picnic basket whose name has
a **long** vowel sound.

A long vowel
sounds like the name of
a vowel—
a, e, i, o, u—
as in rake or seed.

Name _____

Long Vowel Sounds

Make Way for a Worm

Help Wanda Worm find her way through the apple.

Use your crayon to follow the line of words that contain the same vowel sound that you hear in **mouse** and **owl.**

Watch out for Wanda when she gets through the apple.

Don't step on her if she drops out!

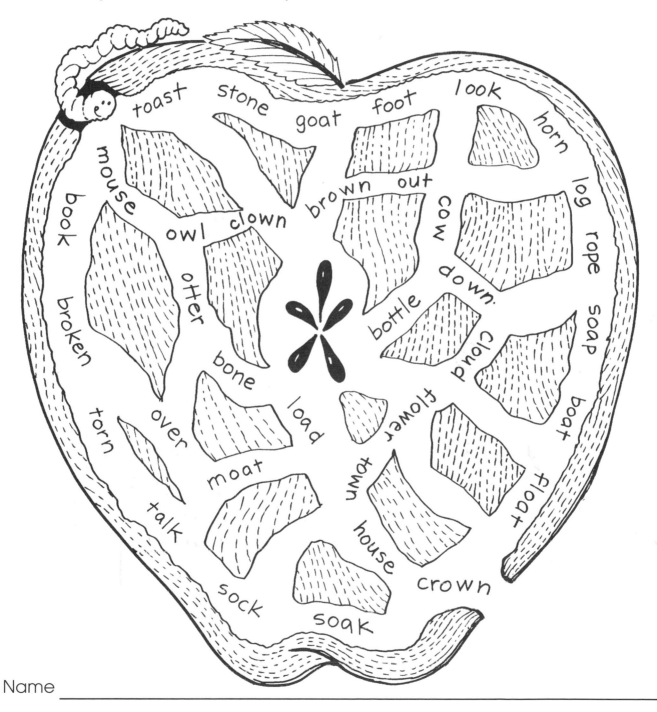

Name _____

Diphthongs (*ow* and *ou*)

The Big Blow

Hang on!

There's a big wind blowing.

Everything is going crazy.

Color **only** the things whose names have **long** vowel sounds.

Can you find 10 things?

   Hint: The words **cape, beet, rice, blow,** and **flute** have long vowel sounds.

Name _____

Long Vowel Combinations

Double the Fun

Each goofy animal has a double **o** or **e** in its name.

Write a word from **Box 1** on the first line in the bubble to name each animal.

You can make the animals say goofy things!

Write a word from **Box 2** on the second line inside the bubble to show what each animal will say.

1.

2.

3.

4.

Read aloud all the words in the boxes. Listen to the vowel sounds.

Color the animals.

Box 1	Box 2
sheep	Boo!
goose	Shoo!
bee	Ooh!
moose	Zoom!
	Eek!
	Toot!
	Beep!
	Coo!
	Seel
	Look!

Name _____

Double Vowels

Silly Questions

Read each silly question.
Underline each word that has a long vowel sound.
Then circle the answer **yes** or **no**.

1. Can a seal cook toast?
   Yes   No

2. Can a fish eat a boat?
   Yes   No

3. Can a toad hop down a road?
   Yes   No

4. Can a bee sleep on the moon?
   Yes   No

5. Can a mouse sleep in a house?
   Yes   No

6. Can a tree read a book?
   Yes   No

7. Will a boot have a room at the zoo?
   Yes   No

8. Can a coat eat a goat?
   Yes   No

Name _____

Long Vowel Combinations

Funny Bunny

Funny Bunny is caught in a cloud of bubbles.
Read the word on each bubble.

Y is a consonant, but sometimes it acts like a vowel.

If **y** sounds like the **long e** at the end of **puppy,** color the bubble **yellow.**

If **y** sounds like the **long i** at the end of **dry,** color the bubble **red.**

buy

messy

pony

pretty

tiny

cry

candy

city

why

try

bunny

my

fry

baby

scary

smelly

fly

Name _____

Shooting Stars

Andy and Mandy are watching shooting stars.
Read the pairs of words in the picture.
If the two words have the **same** meaning, color that space **blue**.
If the two words are **opposites,** color that space **yellow.**

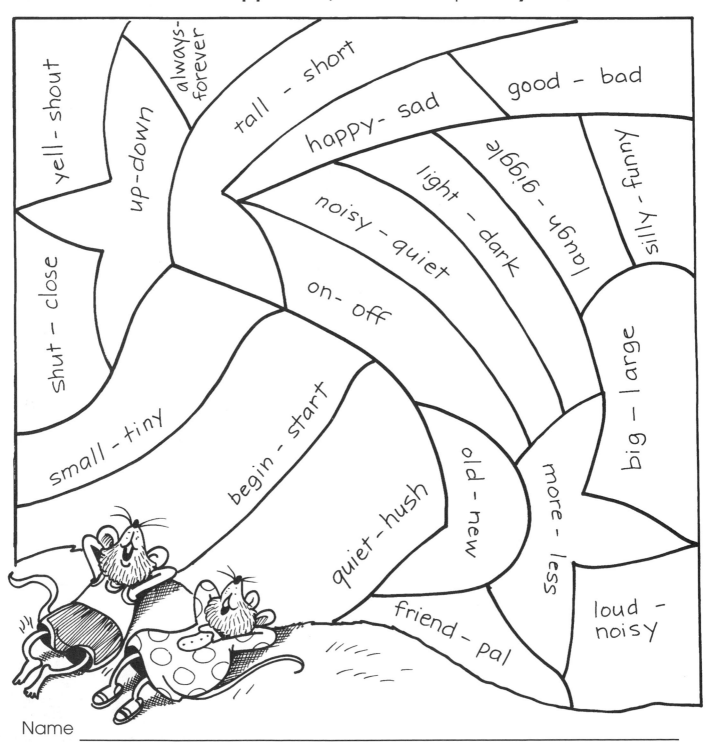

Name _____

Synonyms & Antonyms

Art in the Park

Cool Cat is having an art fair.

He wants his artist friends to join him.

Look at each picture. Read the first word.

Read the second word that sounds the **same**
but is spelled **differently.**

Draw a picture to match the second word.

The people in the park will enjoy your artwork.

Color the pictures.

Name _____

Nouns on the Line

Naming words are called nouns. Nouns name people, animals, things, and places.

Help Blue Bird line up some nouns. Fill each space below with pictures of nouns.

Draw 3 animals, 3 people, 3 things, and 3 places.

animals

people

things

places

Name _____

Make It Proper

Help! Some names are missing from the signs!
Choose a proper noun from the **Name Box** to fill in each space.
Be sure to begin each word with a capital letter.

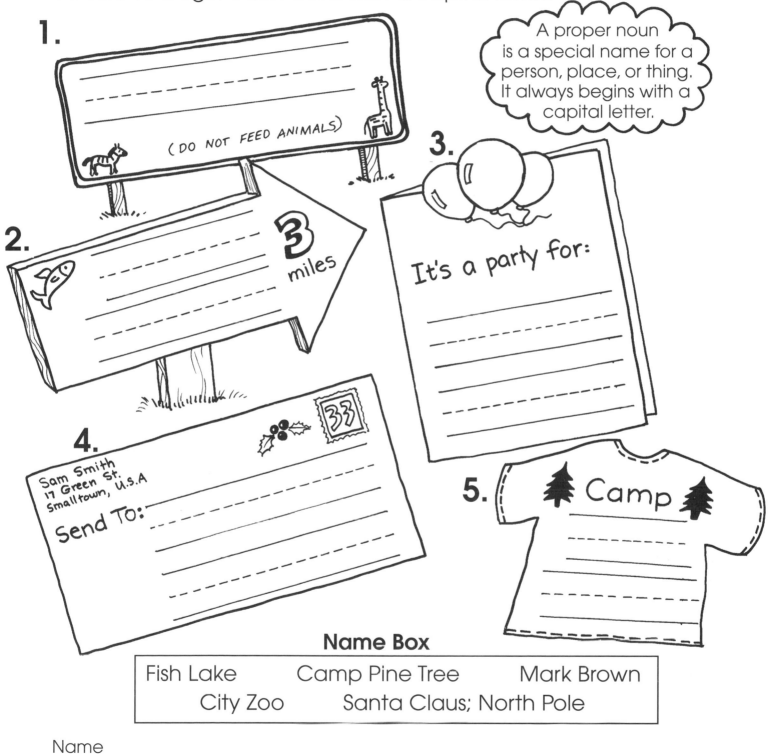

A proper noun is a special name for a person, place, or thing. It always begins with a capital letter.

1.

(DO NOT FEED ANIMALS)

2.

3 miles

3.

It's a party for:

4.

Sam Smith
17 Green St.
Smalltown, U.S.A

Send To:

5.

Camp

Name Box

| Fish Lake | Camp Pine Tree | Mark Brown |
| City Zoo | Santa Claus; North Pole | |

Name

Copyright © 2016 World Book, Inc./
Incentive Publications, Chicago, IL

Proper Nouns

One or More Than One?

The sea creatures are swimming with some underwater nouns. Read the nouns on each picture.

Three of the nouns on each picture are plural.

Put an **X** on the noun in each picture that is not plural.

Plural nouns name more than one of something, like boats or fins.

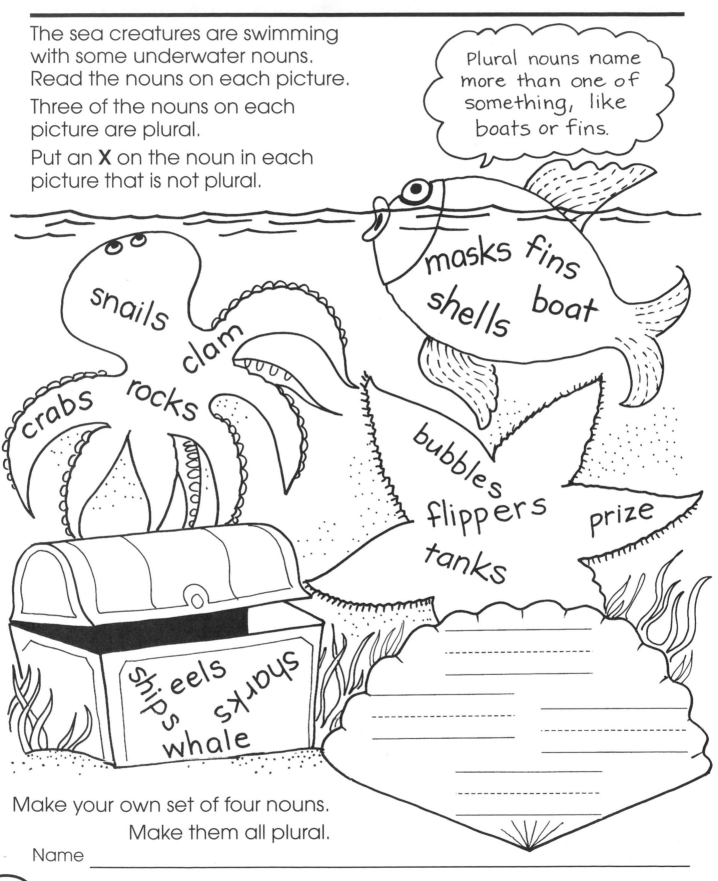

masks fins
shells boat

snails
clam
rocks
crabs

bubbles
flippers
tanks
prize

ships eels
sharks
whale

Make your own set of four nouns.
Make them all plural.

Name _____

Let's Go Hiking!

Let's go hiking with Henry.

First, we will have to help him lace up his boots.

Draw a line from each pair of words to its contraction.

contractions are 2 words squeezed into 1.
I am = I'm
You will = You'll

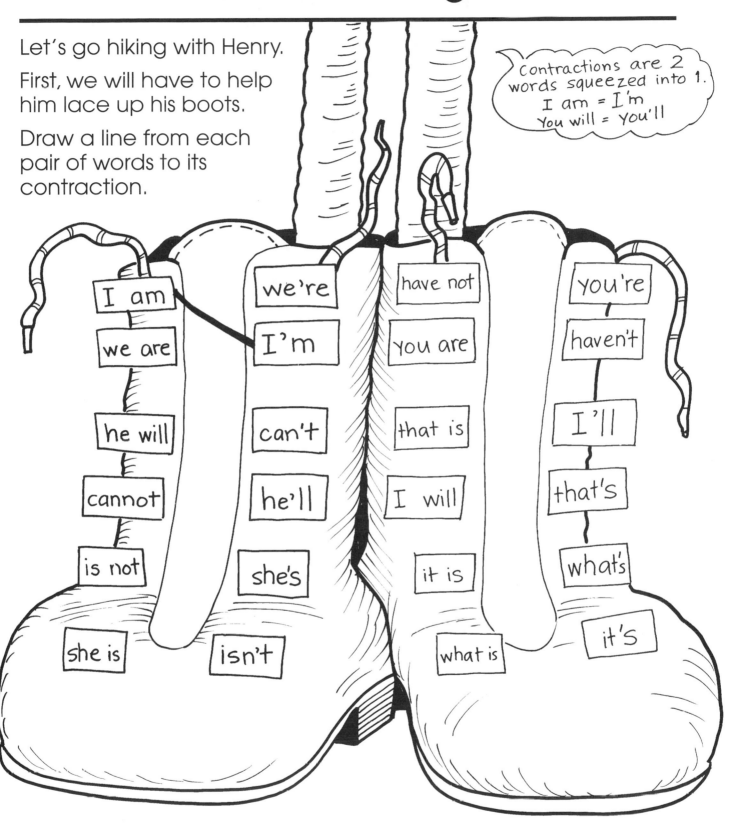

I am
we are
he will
cannot
is not
she is

we're
I'm
can't
he'll
she's
isn't

have not
you are
that is
I will
it is
what is

you're
haven't
I'll
that's
what's
it's

Name _____

Copyright © 2016 World Book, Inc./
Incentive Publications, Chicago, IL

Contractions

Balloons to the Moon!

It's a race to the moon.

Who will win—the rat or the goat?

Look at the pictures on the balloons.

Draw lines to connect any 2 or 3 whose names **rhyme**.

who will get here first? A fat rat in a flat hat, or a goat in a coat with a boat?

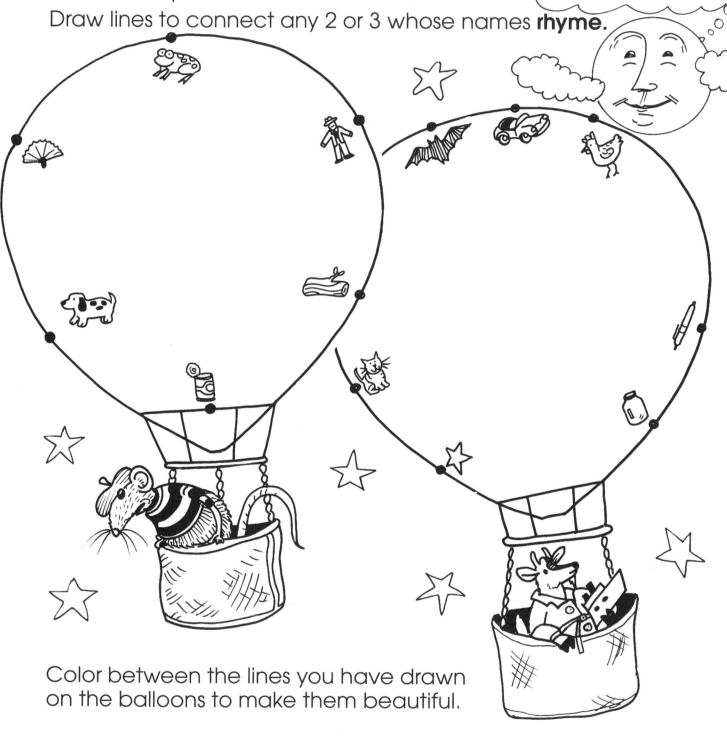

Color between the lines you have drawn on the balloons to make them beautiful.

Name _____

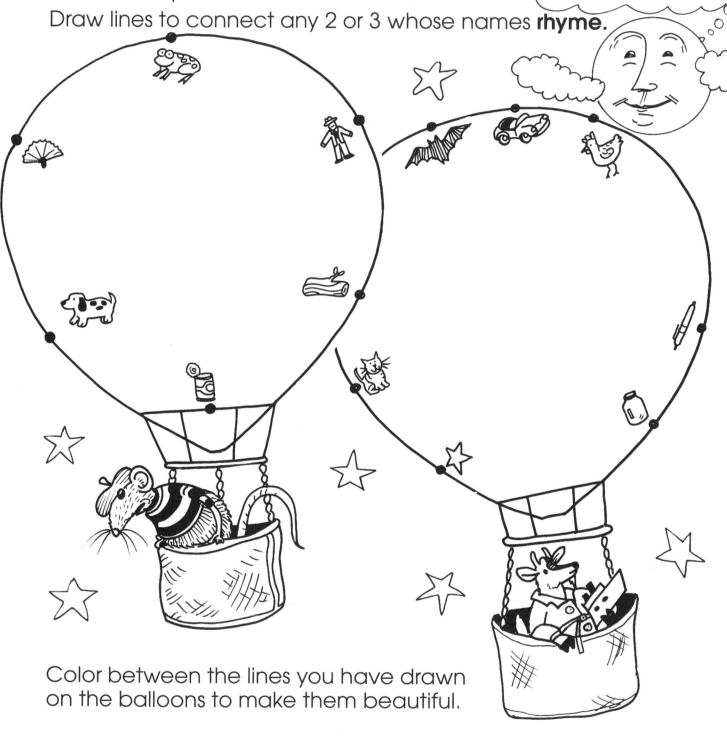

Rhyming Words

Flying Freddy

Did you ever fly on a **compound word?**
Trace the words to show the compound
word Freddy is flying on.

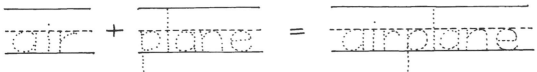

air + plane = airplane

Choose 2 words from the **Word Box** to make a compound
word for each of these.

1. Make a compound word you can eat.

   _____

   -

   _____

2. Make a compound word you can use for a game.

   _____

   -

   _____

3. Make a compound word you can use to grow flowers.

   _____

   -

   _____

4. Make a compound word you can use to clean your teeth.

   _____

   -

   _____

Word Box

base	corn	ball	tooth
green	pop	house	brush

Name _____

Compound Words

Book Covers to Finish

Ollie found some great books in the library.

There is only one problem—the cover pictures are incomplete.

Read the title of each book.

What is missing in the picture?

Complete each picture to match its title.

Name _____

Book Titles

Choose a Title

Today's newspaper has some scary stories about animals in trouble.

Look at the picture of each scene.

Circle the best title for each picture.

1. Fun! Fun! Fun!

Bullfighters Know Best

A Bullfighter in Trouble

3. Look Out Ahead!

A Good Day for Boating

All About Rivers

2. The Storm Is Over

A Big Tornado

The New Car

4. Outdoor Fun

A Good Hike

A Bear Hangs On

Name _____

Warning!

Warnings tell you what to do or what not to do.

Warnings also tell you to watch out for some things.

Look at each picture.

Draw a line to the words that give the warning about that picture.

1.

6.

WARNINGS

2.

DON'T feed the boa!

BEWARE of the cross-eyed moose!

LOOK OUT for smoking dragons!

Caterpillar Crossing!

Leaping Lizards Ahead!

STOP for tap dancing turtles!

5.

3.

4.

Name _____

Captions

Ranch Roundup

The animals at the Lucky Star Ranch are having a good time.

Look at the picture to see what they are doing.

Read all the sentences.

Then draw a line from each sentence to the part of the picture that matches it.

1. The sun is high in the sky.

2. Who left the barn door open?

3. The snake is wearing a hat.

4. Cathy Cow sits on the fence.

5. The horse does rope tricks.

6. Some chickens are loose.

7. Bunny climbs on the fence.

8. The mountains are high.

9. Whose shirt has spots?

10. A rock is a place to rest.

Name _____

Match Sentences to Pictures

The Dress-Up Party

These fun-loving animals are all dressed up for a party.
They have decided to dress up like each other!
Look at the picture to see who is in each costume.
Draw a line to the correct answer.

1. Which animal dressed up like a spider?   **mouse**

2. Which animal dressed up like a duck?   **chicken**

3. Which animal dressed up like a chicken?   **frog**

4. Which animal dressed up like a rabbit?   **spider**

5. Which animal dressed up like a mouse?   **rabbit**

6. Which animal dressed up like a frog?   **duck**

Name _____

The Good Morning Machine

Connie's machine gets her up in the morning.

It helps her do many things.

Look at this funny machine.

Then write the correct letter to answer each question.

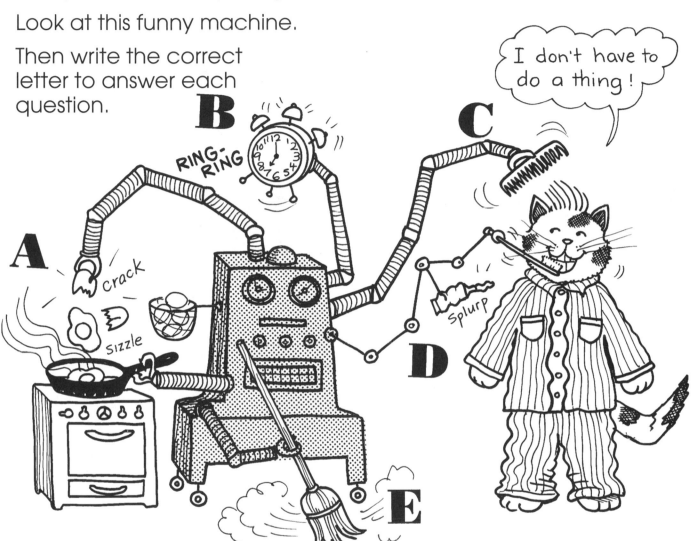

1. Which part of the machine combs Connie's hair? _____

2. Which part of the machine cooks her breakfast? _____

3. Which part of the machine sweeps the floor? _____

4. Which part of the machine wakes her up? _____

5. Which part of the machine gives her toothpaste? _____

Name _____

Illustrations

Big Bad Al

Big Al does some bad things.
What has he done this time?
Read the poster about him to find out.

Wanted: Big Bad AL.

Grrrrrr

Cookies

Wanted for stealing cookies and
scaring the neighbors
REWARD: 100 cookies

Circle the correct answer to each question.

1. What kind of animal is Al? **an alligator** **a grasshopper**

2. What size is Al? **small** **big**

3. Did Big Al steal cookies? **Yes** **No**

4. Did Big Al steal crackers? **Yes** **No**

5. Did Big Al get scared? **Yes** **No**

6. Who did Al scare? **the doctor** **the cookies** **the neighbors**

7. Would you like to find Big Al and get the reward? **Yes** **No**

Name _____

A Pail on a Porcupine

Pokey Porcupine has his head stuck in a pail.

He is trying to find his way home.

Finish the sentences to follow Pokey's trail.

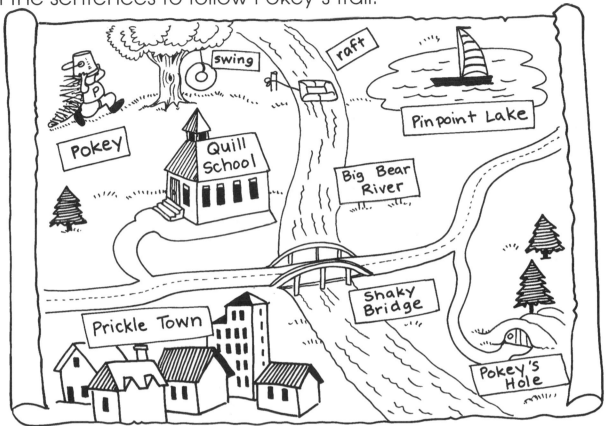

Circle the correct answer.

1. Pokey passes the swing outside (**Quill School**   **Pickle Town**).

2. He rides a raft across the Big Bear (**River**   **Lake**).

3. He almost falls into (**Pinpoint**   **Prickle**) Lake.

4. Pokey crosses the river on (**Quill**   **Shaky**) Bridge.

5. He wanders around the streets of (**Shaky**   **Prickle**) Town.

6. Finally, he crosses the bridge again and finds his own home, which is called _____.

Use a red crayon to draw a trail to each place Pokey went.

Name _____

Find Information on a Map

How Tall Is Tall?

Did you know that giraffes are the world's tallest animals?
The giraffe and some tall friends are getting measured.
Look at the chart and answer the questions.

Circle the right answer.

1. Is the moose taller than the elephant?
   yes   no

2. Which is shorter, the snake or the bear?
   bear   rattlesnake

3. Which animal is as tall as the gorilla?
   rattlesnake   moose

4. Is the giraffe exactly 5 feet taller than the bear?   **yes   no**

5. Which animal is 8 feet tall?
   gorilla   moose   elephant

Name _____

Find Information on a Graph

A Dear Goldie Letter

Baby Bear was not happy that Goldilocks visited his house.

He wrote her a letter to tell her what he thought.

His letter is mixed up.

Help him get the lines in the right order.

Put **1, 2, 3, 4,** and **5** in the boxes to show the right order.

She didn't even say good-bye...

- [ ] You broke my chair!
- [ ] Sadly yours, Baby Bear
- [ ] Dear Goldie,
- [ ] You ran away!
- [ ] You came to my house.

Dear Goldie,

Write the letter the way it should be.

1. _____

2. _____

3. _____

4. _____

5. _____

Name _____

Hunting for Treasure

There's a treasure waiting for Henry and Hannah to find.
But how will they find it?
Choose from the sentences in the **Sentence Box** to complete the problems below.

Write 2 things they should do **before** they hunt for the treasure.

1. _____

2. _____

Write 2 things they should do **during** the treasure hunt.

1. _____

2. _____

Write 2 things they should do **after** they find the treasure.

1. _____

2. _____

Keep digging!

Sentence Box

Dig for the treasure.	Find some shovels.
Follow the map.	Get a treasure map.
Take the treasure home.	Enjoy the treasure.

Name _____

Raining Cats & Dogs!

It started out as a quiet summer day.
Before long, Missie Mole was in the middle of a storm.
The sentences that tell about the storm are out of order.
Number them in the right order (**1, 2, 3, 4, 5, 6,** and **7**).

☐ Then, the rain changed to cats and dogs.

☐ The storm was over.

☐ Missie was enjoying her nap when she heard thunder.

☐ The cats and dogs barked and screeched as they came down.

☐ Finally, the cats and dogs stopped pouring down.

☐ After the thunder started, small drops of rain began to fall.

☐ Missie woke up. She had been dreaming!

Draw 2 more cats and 2 more dogs pouring down in the storm.

Name _____

A Monster in the Closet

Mattie Mouse dreamed that there was a monster hiding in her closet!

See what the monster looks like.

Follow the directions.

1. Give the monster 3 green eyes.

2. Color the horns on its head red.

3. Draw a big mouth on the monster.

4. Draw 4 big teeth in the mouth.

5. Put 1 long nose on the monster.

6. Put funny ears on the monster.

7. Color the toenails orange.

8. Draw 10 purple spots on the body.

9. Finish the monster any way you like.

10. Give the monster a name.

Write the name on the line below the monster.

Don't worry.
It's not a real monster.
It's only a dream.

_____

Name _____

A Jar of Creepy Crawlers

Felix Frog loves to collect insects!
Look at the things in the jar.
Follow the directions to color the insects.

Color the butterflies orange.
Color the ladybugs red.
Color the snails purple.
Color the worms brown.
Color the beetles green.
Color the ants black.
Color the spiders blue.

Name _____

Out to Sea

This is a short, funny old poem.
Have you heard it before?
Read the poem, and write your answers to the questions.

A sailor went to sea
To see what he could see
And all that he could see
Was sea, sea, sea!!

1. Who went to sea? Sailor

2. Which 2 words in the poem sound the same but do not mean the same thing? see / sea

3. What did the sailor see? sea

4. Look at the picture. What did the sailor NOT see?
The octopus.

Name _____

The Big Squeeze

Anaconda is a big word.

Read to find out what an anaconda is.

Then answer the questions.

Say
anna-kon-dah

Anacondas are very BIG snakes!

They are green with black spots.

They live in the rain forest.

Anacondas squeeze their food!

These snakes can grow to be very long and very thick.

1. Are anacondas big or small?

Big

2. What do these snakes look like?

Green, with black spots.

3. Where do anacondas live?

Rain forest

4. What do they do with their food?

Squeeze their food.

Name _____

Find Facts & Details

A Teeny Tiny Poem

Here is a teeny tiny poem about a teeny tiny man.
Read the poem and draw a picture of
Teeny Tiny Jack in the circle.
Then answer the questions.

Jack Hall
He is so small,
A mouse could eat him,
Hat and all.

Draw Jack here.
Don't forget his hat!

1. Who is so small? _Jack Hall_

2. Who could eat him? _Mouse_

3. Write the word in the poem that rhymes with cat.
Hat

4. Does Jack have a hat? _____

5. Write one word that rhymes with small. _Fall_

Name _____

Create Illustrations

Cool Ears, Hot Ears

Did you know that big ears can keep an animal cooler?

Read about these animal cousins to find out why.

Then look at the pictures and answer the questions.

jackrabbit   arctic hare   desert fox   arctic fox

> **An animal can lose body heat through its ears and tail.**
> **If the ears or tail are small, it doesn't lose much heat.**
> **This helps to keep the animal warm in cold weather.**
> **If the ears or tail are long, it will lose more heat.**
> **Losing heat keeps the animal cooler in hot weather.**

1. Which 2 animals do you think live where it is cold? (Circle 2.)

   arctic fox   desert fox   arctic hare   jackrabbit

   Why do you think that?

   _____

   -

   _____

2. Which 2 animals live where it is hot? (Circle 2.)

   arctic fox   desert fox   arctic hare   jackrabbit

   Why do you think that?

   _____

   -

   _____

Name _____

Inference

Poems to Eat

These are two of Tonya Turtle's favorite food poems.

Which one do you like best?

Follow the directions, and answer the questions.

Three slices of bread

Two bits of cheese

Three tomatoes

Five onions

And mustard, if you please

A hunk of turkey

A chunk of Jello

A head of lettuce

Some ketchup, too

I'll taste my sandwich now

Would you like to, too?

Nice and drippy

Slurpy

Creamy

Icy

Cold

On your tongue

Chocolate ripple

Ice Cream Cone

1. Give each poem a title. Write it on the line above the poem.

2. Tell why you like one of the poems.

- -

3. Which words did you like in the sandwich poem?

- -

4. Which words made the ice cream sound tasty?

- -

Name _____

Personal Response

Sound-Alikes

Mazie and Morris Mouse came to say good-bye to their friends.
The boat is full of sound-alike words.
Read the sentences.
Each sentence has two words that sound alike.
Circle the correct word for each sentence.

1. Good! The (**son   sun**) is shining.

2. Let's (**peak   peek**) in the window!

3. We hope it won't (**rein   rain**).

4. The ocean is very (**blue   blew**).

5. They will sail on the (**see   sea**).

6. Friends are saying good- (**bye   buy**).

7. (**Eight   Ate**) mice are leaving.

8. (**Ant   Aunt**) Zelda is leaving.

9. The baby is going, (**to   too**).

Name _____

Homonyms

Some Very Chilly Letters

Paula Penguin has a riddle on the outside of her igloo.

The riddle is: **"What are the two coldest letters?"**

To find the answer to the riddle, follow the directions.

If the two words in each block are opposites,
color the block black.

If the two words in each block are not opposites,
leave the block white.

What 2 letters give the answer? ___ ___

Name _____

Antonyms

A Letter Riddle

Bruno Bear has a word puzzle on his honey jar.

Read the two words in each puzzle piece.

If the two words mean the same thing, color in the space.

If the two words are opposites, do not color the space.

old young
mean kind
sweet sour
soft hard
good bad
in out
right wrong
stop go
like hate
sleepy tired
icy cold
tall long
happy sad
same different
nice kind
quick fast
run jog
true false
stop halt
near far
old new
shut close
hurry rush
top bottom
thin fat
tiny small
big small
up down
friend pal

Bruno also has a riddle in the puzzle.

It is: **"What 2 letters hold nothing?"** The answer to the riddle is ___ ___.

Name _____

A Really Big Guy!

What should you call a 2,000 pound gorilla?

To find out, follow the code to color the spaces.

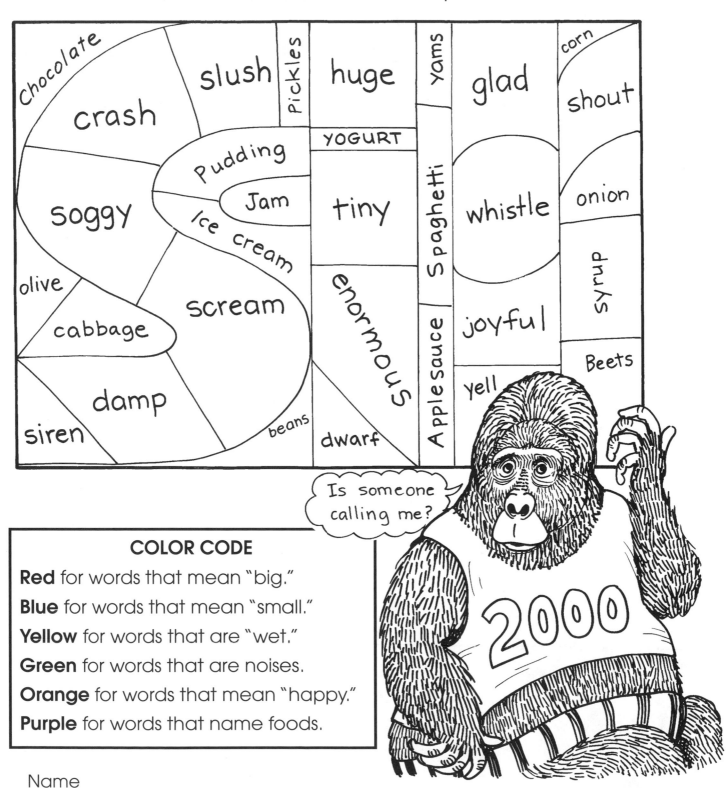

Chocolate • crash • slush • Pickles • huge • Yams • glad • corn • shout

Pudding • YOGURT • Spaghetti • whistle • onion

soggy • Jam • tiny • syrup

Ice cream • scream • enormous • Applesauce • joyful • Beets

olive • cabbage • yell

damp • siren • beans • dwarf

Is someone calling me?

2000

COLOR CODE

Red for words that mean "big."

Blue for words that mean "small."

Yellow for words that are "wet."

Green for words that are noises.

Orange for words that mean "happy."

Purple for words that name foods.

Name _____

Word Classification & Meaning

Cousins with Ears

Jack Rabbit and Sam, the snowshoe rabbit, are cousins.

They are alike because they are both rabbits.

They look different, however, and they live in different places.

Help them find their ways to their homes.

Follow the "hot" words to Jack's warm home.

Follow the "cold" words to Sam's cold home.

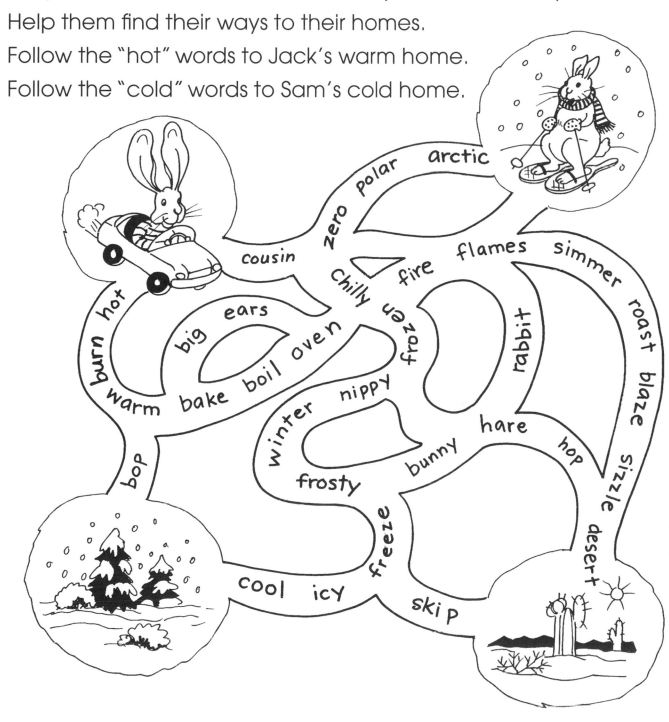

Name _____

Synonyms & Antonyms

On a Dark Night

What is happening at the campfire?

Read the sentences below to find out what these campers are doing on a cold, dark night.

Circle the best choice for the missing word.

1. It was a dark and scary (**night**   **day**).

2. The campers were (**sleeping**   **sitting**) around the fire.

3. They were telling (**funny**   **scary**) stories.

4. The (**wind**   **snow**) was blowing around them.

5. Some campers saw a (**little**   **huge**) shadow behind them.

6. The shadow belonged to a (**bear**   **mouse**   **rabbit**).

Name _____

Context

Sign Painters Needed

Simon, the sign painter, would like some help.

Look at the two choices of words above each sign.

Choose the right words to go on each sign.

Write them on the signs.

WET PAINT or WET PRINT

STOP or STOOP

QUITE or QUIET

FOR SALE or SEAL

DOGS WORKING or DOGS WALKING

NO PARKING or NO BARKING

Name _____

Letter to a Friend

Pretend that you have just been to the Apple Pie Circus.
Write a letter to a friend to tell about it.
First, draw a picture of something from the circus.
Then tell your friend what you saw at the circus.

Dear _____,

I went to _____

I saw _____

_____

Love, _____

Name _____

Writing: Letter

Poster Problems

Poppy, the poster painter, is making a poster for the circus.
He is too tired to finish it, and he needs your help!
Think of the words to write and finish the poster for Poppy.
His sign will tell you things that need to be on the poster.

The Apple Pie Circus

things to put on the Circus Poster:

Time
Day
Place
Cost
And a great big picture

Name _____

Writing: Poster

The Magic Circus Mirror

Look in the magic circus mirror.

What would you like to be in the circus?

Draw a picture of yourself in the mirror.

Draw yourself to be anything or anyone you wish.

Then write about it on the lines.

I want to be

because

Name _____

Writing: Imaginative Piece

Yummy Tummy Stuff

There is some tasty food at a circus.
How does it look? How does it smell?
How does it taste? How does it feel?
Try to describe some circus food.
Fill in each blank with your ideas.

POPCORN

looks _____

tastes _____

sounds _____

ICE CREAM CONE

tastes _____

feels _____

COTTON CANDY

feels _____

looks _____

SODA POP

tastes _____

feels _____

smells _____

Name _____

Writing: Similes

Fantastic Circus Tricks

What fantastic tricks!

The circus performers make everyone happy.

Read about the tricks.

Then write a title for every story.

_____

- -

_____

Be careful!

It is a long way down to the ground!

The tightrope walker has a dangerous job.

We hope she does not slip and fall.

_____

- -

_____

I only have one wheel.

It is hard to balance.

But I am pretty good.

Would you like to try my unicycle?

_____

- -

_____

I clap my flippers.

I balance balls on my nose.

If I do my tricks,

I will get some tasty fish!

Name _____

Writing: Titles

Fantastic Circus Tricks, cont.

_____

- - - - - - - - - - - - - - - - - -

What a bouncy ride!

The bareback rider does not fall.

She smiles as she rides the fancy horse.

What is her name?

_____

- - - - - - - - - - - - - - - - - -

Such a big animal!

Elmo stands up high on his back legs.

His trick is so hard.

When he is finished, he will get peanuts for a treat.

_____

- - - - - - - - - - - - - - - - - -

The dogs are funny.

They can stand on each other.

What a good dog tower they make!

Name _____

Use with page 82.

Writing: Titles

Silly Circus Sentences

Gino wants to tell a friend about some funny things that happened today.

He has written parts of some sentences.

Finish his sentences.

Use the words in the bubble.

Make the sentences very silly!

big toe   zucchini
snake   porcupine
dishes   ears   elbow
popsicle cactus dog food
red ants   belly button
toad   taco   dandelion

1 Hubba stood on his _____ .

2 The elephant swallowed a _____ .

3 "Don't sit on that _____ "
.

4 Lolly jumped over a _____ .

5 Mighty Mo cooked _____ .

6 Clowns hate to wash _____ .

7 Zebras love to smell _____ .

Name _____

Writing: Sentences

The Great Rondo

Meet Rondo the Magician! Poof! Whizz! Shazaamm!

He has some circus words you can use to make magic.

Read the words in the cloud of smoke.

Use some of these words and some of your own.

Write one statement, one question, and one exclamation.

Abracadabra!

circus   music   pop
elephants   tricks   roar
seals   balls   scary   juggle
bareback rider   clowns
Big Top   dogs   lions
merry-go-round
bears   tigers   trapeze

1

2

3

Name _____

Writing: Sentences

The Big Top's Top 10

What do you want to see at the circus?

The twins are trying to choose the 10 most important things to see.

They have each written a list.

Write your list of the top 10 things you want to see at the circus.

Your List

1. _____
2. _____
3. _____
4. _____
5. _____
6. _____
7. _____
8. _____
9. _____
10. _____

Bubba's List

sawdust

flags

popcorn

elephants

peanuts

unicycle

ropes

trailers

ice cream

dogs

Hubba's List

costumes

red noses

flowers

hats

funny shoes

feathers

face paint

wigs

ribbons

candy

Name _____

Writing: Lists

Good Words for a Circus

So many things happen at the circus!
Read these four circus words.
What do they make you think about?
Write some more words to tell about each
of the four words below.

ELEPHANT

_____
- - - - - - - - - - - - - - - - - - -
_____
- - - - - - - - - - - - - - - - - - -
_____

CLOWN

_____
- - - - - - - - - - - - - - - - - - -
_____
- - - - - - - - - - - - - - - - - - -
_____

TIGER

_____
- - - - - - - - - - - - - - - - - - -
_____
- - - - - - - - - - - - - - - - - - -
_____

TRICKS

_____
- - - - - - - - - - - - - - - - - - -
_____
- - - - - - - - - - - - - - - - - - -
_____

Name _____

Writing: Descriptive Words

Those Daring Dogs!

Daring performers! Beautiful animals! Delightful clowns!
So many wonderful things make up a circus.
There are many circus words in this puzzle.
Connect them in ABC order to make a circus picture.

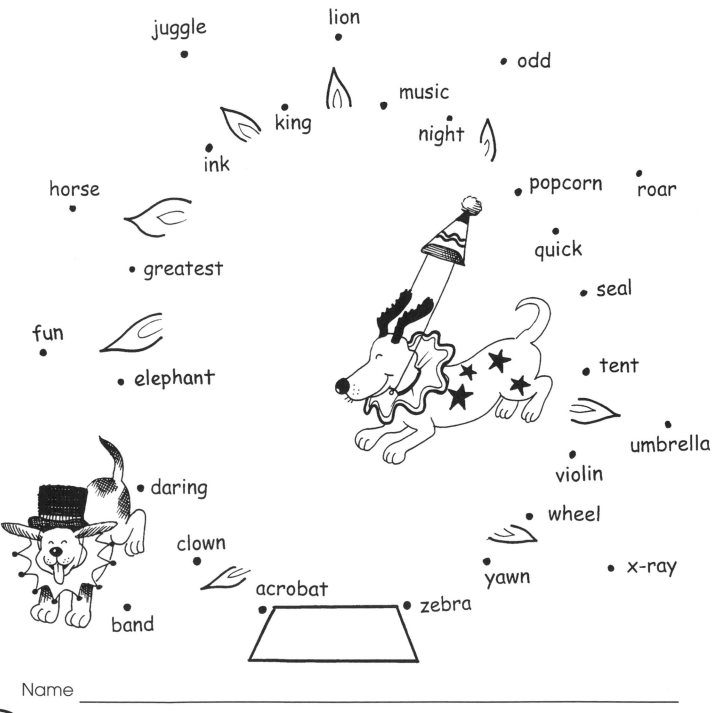

juggle

lion

odd

music

king

night

ink

horse

popcorn

roar

greatest

quick

seal

fun

elephant

tent

umbrella

daring

violin

clown

wheel

acrobat

yawn

x-ray

band

zebra

Name _____

Spotlight on Circus Words

Some circus words are in the spotlight tonight.

These words are hidden in the puzzle.

Look at the picture.

Fill in the blanks with letters to complete the words.

Then find each word in the puzzle, and color the squares that spell the word.

b__ __r

___ion

c__m__l

mo__k__y

C	L	O	W	N	R
A	I	R	J	B	X
M	O	N	K	E	Y
E	N	N	V	A	Q
L	Z	E	B	R	A

ze__ra

cl__w__

Name _____

Funny, Funny!

Zilla loves funny jokes, but she forgets punctuation marks!
Can you help her?

Read the jokes and put the punctuation marks where they belong.

Use a **period (.), question mark (?),** or **exclamation point (!).**

Draw a happy face in the circle at the beginning of the joke if you think the joke is funny.

1. Why did the clown throw the clock out the window She wanted to see time fly

2. Why are fish so smart They are smart because they live in schools

3. What do you call a dog at the beach A hot dog

4. Why is 6 afraid of 7 He's afraid because 7 8 9

5. Why is 2 + 2 = 5 like your left hand It's not right

6. How did the ocean say good-bye It waved

Name _____

A Letter From a Fan

The Flying Ferelli Brothers got a fan letter from a frog named Happy.

Happy has some trouble writing his sentences.

Read his letter and circle his mistakes in punctuation.

Write the corrected letter on the lines.

Dear Flip. Flap. and Flop.
Hello? My name is Happy Frog?
I live in Stinky Swamp! I love your act,
I want to join the circus,
Do you need another brother!
                    Your friend, Happy

I could be a star!

Name _____

Punctuation Marks

Flip, Flap, & Flop!

Every exclamation ends with an exclamation point!

The Flying Ferelli Brothers are fabulous on the flying trapeze!

Flip, Flap, and Flop are performing for the audience.

Read what everyone is saying.

Put a big exclamation point at the end of each exclamation.

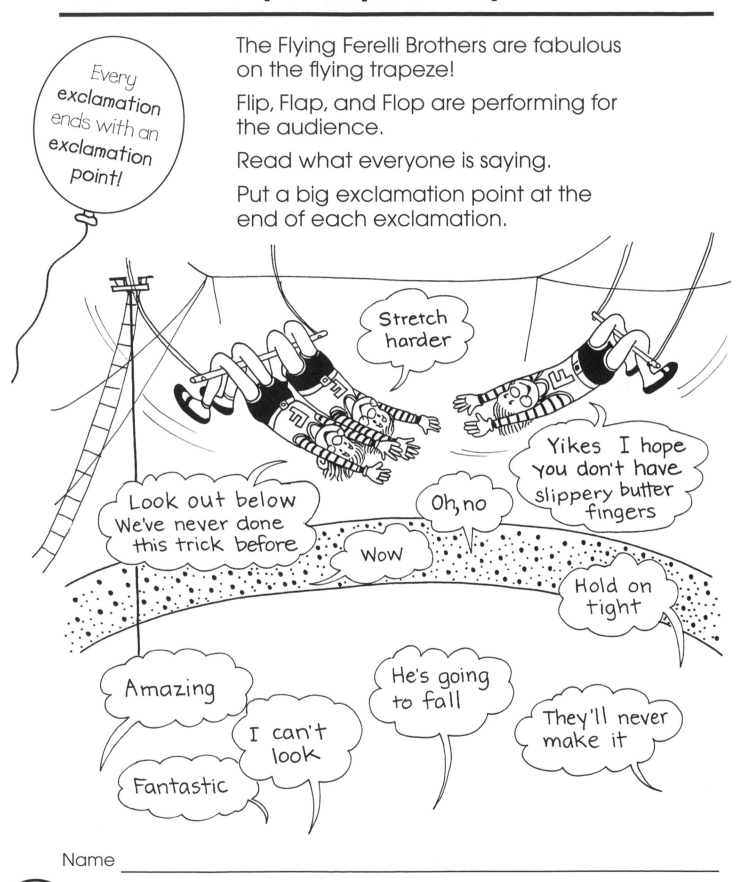

Name _____

Punctuation: Exclamation Points

Meet the Cook

Cookie Clown is the cook for the animals in the circus stables.

She makes a special recipe for each animal.

Read each animal's food list.

Put a comma after each food in the list except the last one.

Put a **comma** after every word in a list except the last one.

1. Elephants like lots and lots of hay grass leaves fruit and branches.

2. Chimps get some nuts leaves honey ants and bananas.

3. Lions eat roast chops liver and bones for their teeth.

4. Seals love things from the sea like fish eels squid and clams.

Cookie's Surprise:
hay, honey,
liver, eels,
and sugar.

Name _____

Punctuation: Commas

Balloons for Sale

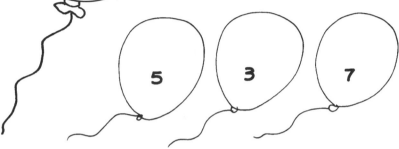

Every **question** should end with a question mark **(?)**.

"Would you buy a red or blue balloon?" asks Zilla.

Read the sentences about the balloons.

Add a **question mark (?)** if the sentence asks a question and a **period (.)** if it is a statement.

Color the matching balloon red if it is a **question.**

Color the matching balloon blue if it is a **statement.**

5 **3** **7**

1. Are these balloons for sale

2. How much do they cost

3. Does Zilla sell blue ones

4. Who wants a red one

5. I don't want to pop them

6. Clowns like balloons

7. Does Zilla have six balloons

8. Did you bring money

    Try to answer the questions.

Name _____

Punctuation: Question Marks

Crazy Mirrors

Ha, ha! Ho, ho! The mirrors make these clowns look weird!
Read what each one is saying as he or she
looks in the mirror.

Each one is saying two sentences. Put a
capital letter at the beginning of each
sentence and name.

Put a big **period (.)** at the end of each sentence.

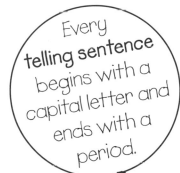

Every **telling sentence** begins with a capital letter and ends with a period.

1. I look like a skinny guy from outer space all I need is green skin

2. I am so short I could fit into a mouse's clothes

3. I look so wide I could be a beach ball

4. hey, this is cool i'm mighty mo the super hero

Name _____

Punctuation: Periods

Plenty of Punctuation

Punctuation marks *make writing easier to understand.*

Klaus the clown is full of punctuation marks!

So is the circus tent!

Many other circus things have punctuation marks, too.

Color everything with **periods (.)** red.

Color everything with **question marks (?)** blue.

Color everything with **commas (,)** purple.

Color everything with **exclamation points (!)** green.

Name _____

The Man with Tattoos

Tiny has a story tattooed on his arm, but it has a lot of mistakes.

Some letters should be capitals.

Other letters are capitals and should not be.

Find the mistakes on Tiny and correct them.

Mom

Tiny

Yippee! I am such a Lucky guy.
I am Going to pick Roses and Pink tulips
with my mom Today. I think pink is The prettiest
Color in the World. we are going to Go to a tea
Party, too. miss sherry twinkletoes is giving the
party. she is my Best friend.

Name _____

Capitalization Errors

A Riddle with Teeth

Begin every sentence with a *capital letter.*

I really need one.

Very nice, very neat

Has teeth, but cannot eat.

Find the answer to the riddle! Here's how.

Read each sentence and find the letter that should be a capital.

Write the letter in the box. Make it a capital letter.

Then write it on the matching line below.

☐ 1. ten terrible toads tackled the tot.

☐ 2. old blue toast is tasty.

☐ 3. i want to shake my sillies out!

☐ 4. can you wiggle your big ears?

☐ 5. i like purple green beans.

☐ 6. beware of slow grasshoppers.

☐ 7. a great big daisy slept on the couch.

☐ 8. my mother loves pink jelly beans.

☐ 9. slow down, Mr. Turtle!

___ ___ ___ ___ ___ ___ ___ ___ ___!
 3   1   5   9   7   4   2   8   6

Name _____

Capitalization in Sentences

Private Thoughts

These circus folks are thinking private thoughts.
Read what they are thinking.

Circle the proper nouns that should have capital letters.

Write the capital letter above each word you circle.

A **proper noun** is a special name. It begins with a capital letter.

1. flying fred is my favorite act in the apple pie circus.

2. I love the clown circus in paris, france.

3. lolly and I always go to the zoo in miami, florida.

4. My brother, zorba, will be in a parade in july in san francisco.

5. I'm going to take tracy and stacy to the circus on wednesday.

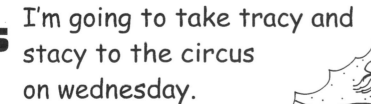

Name _____

Capitalization of Proper Nouns

Lots of Mail

Names, street names, cities, and countries begin with *capital letters*.

The circus performers have family and friends all over the world. They have lots of mail for the mail carrier to take to the post office.

Read the name and address on each piece of mail.

Many of the letters should be capitals.

Circle these letters, and put the capital letters above them.

Mail call!

sir tiny taylor
300 blackberry street
bramble, england

mr. lee chen
201 jade road
beijing, china

mrs. jane hopper
501 rye lane
sweet home, oregon

Rush   urgent !!   santa claus   north pole

mrs. donna prima
412 main street
toledo, ohio

return to:
z. zucchini
590 palm st.
winter park, florida

Name _____

Capitalization in Addresses

Lovely Lolly

Lovely Lolly needs help lacing up her new flowered coat.

Both of her hands are full of circus treats.

Draw a line from each pair of words to the matching contraction.

Color Lolly's pretty coat and hat.

A **contraction** is two words squeezed together to make one. I + am = I'm

we are ○	○ I'm
she is ○	○ we're
I am ○	○ she's
is not ○	○ won't
can not ○	○ can't
will not ○	○ isn't
does not ○	○ didn't
did not ○	○ I'll
I will ○	○ doesn't

Name _____

Contractions

Gina the Gypsy

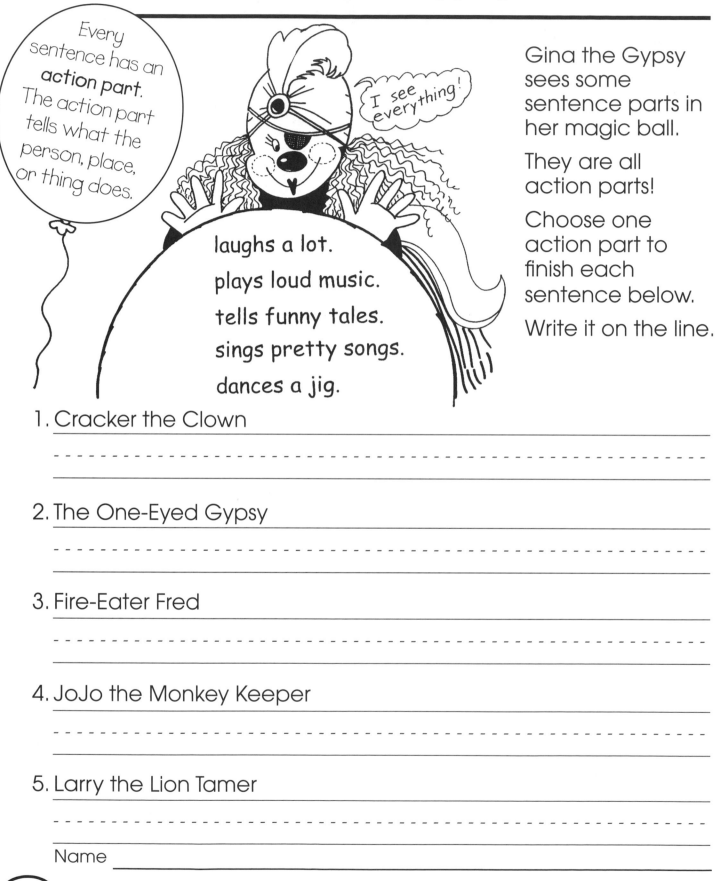

Every sentence has an **action part**. The action part tells what the person, place, or thing does.

I see everything!

laughs a lot.

plays loud music.

tells funny tales.

sings pretty songs.

dances a jig.

Gina the Gypsy sees some sentence parts in her magic ball.

They are all action parts!

Choose one action part to finish each sentence below.

Write it on the line.

1. Cracker the Clown

- -

2. The One-Eyed Gypsy

- -

3. Fire-Eater Fred

- -

4. JoJo the Monkey Keeper

- -

5. Larry the Lion Tamer

- -

Name

Action Part of a Sentence

Inside a Riddle

Riddle me, riddle me.

What is that?

Over the head,

And under my hat?

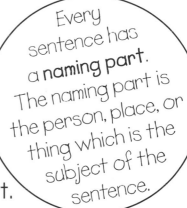

What is the answer to the riddle?

Read each sentence, and circle the naming part.

Write the first letter of the naming part you circled on the right line at the bottom of the page.

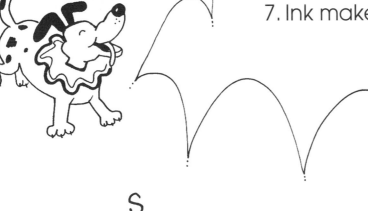

The first one is done for you.

1. (Snakes) sleep all day.

2. Ants love jelly beans.

3. Robert eats wiggly worms.

4. Hippos hate hot soup.

5. Holly hangs out with hopping toads.

6. I fly foxes to France.

7. Ink makes you blue!

__ __ S __ __ __ __ __
4   7 1   5   2   6   3

Name _____

Naming Part of a Sentence

Riding High

*Every sentence has a **naming part** and an **action part**.*

The twins love to ride on all the rides.

Their favorite rides are the ones that go very high!

Read these sentences that tell about the rides.

Draw a green line under the **naming part** of each sentence.

Draw a blue circle around the **action part** of each sentence.

1. The rocket blaster shoots through the air.

2. The small cars fly past the twins.

3. The toy planes buzz around and around.

4. The roller coaster goes racing by.

5. The Ferris wheel touches the treetops.

6. The painted ponies prance up and down.

Name _____

Sentence Parts

The Ringmaster

Rollo, the ringmaster, shouts out the exciting events in the circus show.

Can you tell what kind of sentences he is yelling out?

Put a **period (.)** at the end of each statement.

Put a **question mark (?)** at the end of each question.

Put an **exclamation point (!)** at the end of each exclamation.

A statement ends with a .
A question ends with a ?
An exclamation ends with an !

Ladies and Gentlemen!

1. Come one, come all
2. See the greatest show on Earth
3. We have big baby elephants
4. Have you seen the purple painted lady
5. Watch Zilla zoom in her tiny sports car
6. The acts are so exciting
7. Wow! Come and see us
8. Ride the giant Ferris wheel
9. Did you bring your family
10. Don't forget to buy popcorn
11. Try the cotton candy
12. Watch the spinning plates

Cheers!
Hurray!
Bravo!

Bring out the elephants.

Hurray!   Bravo!   Good Show!   clap   clap   Yahoo!

Name _____

Statements, Questions, & Exclamations

Dunk That Clown!

Bozo is yelling and calling people funny names.

He wants them to throw balls and try to dunk him in the water tank. Read each sentence.

If a sentence is an exclamation, put an **exclamation point (!)** at the end.

Then color the ball that matches the number of the sentence.

Exclamations show that someone is excited, angry, or scared. They end with an !

Na-na! Missed me!

1. Oops, you missed, Pie Face

2. Hey, Pumpkin Ears, go home

3. Dunk me, Slow Poke

4. Oh no, not you again

5. The little boy threw a ball

6. Will he fall in

7. Ouch

8. Watch it, Big Nose

Name _____

A Fishy Act

Flipper and his friend get a reward for doing tricks. Follow the directions to find Flipper and his friend. Color 8 shapes that have **nouns** **(naming words)** in them **yellow.** Color 7 shapes that have **verbs** **(action words)** in them **purple.** Color 11 shapes that have **adjectives** **(describing words)** in them **green.**

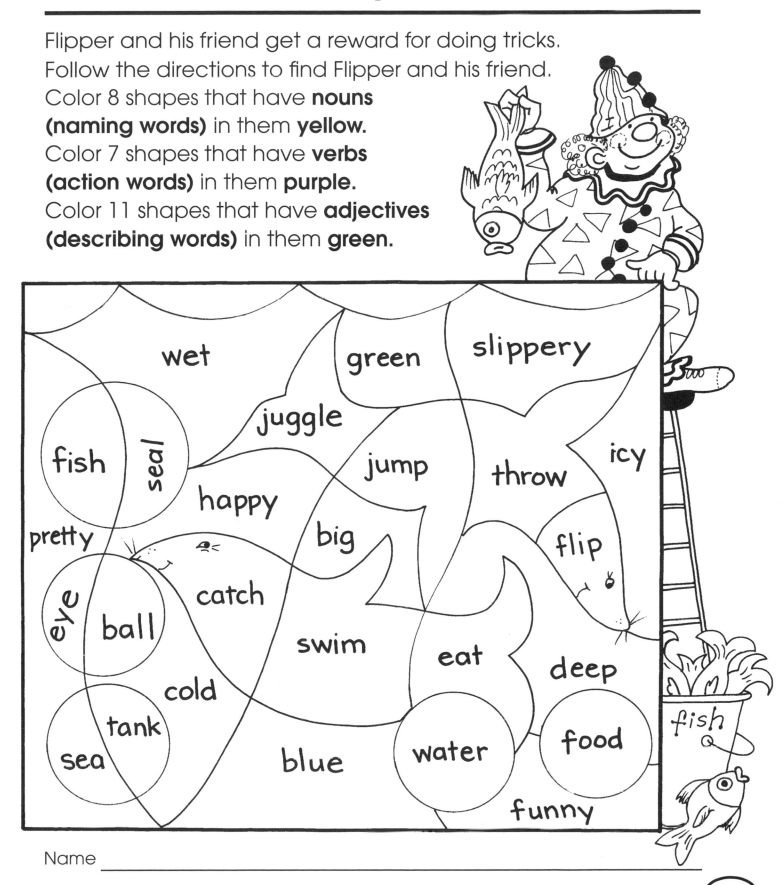

Name _____

Nouns, Verbs, & Adjectives

My Hat Is Fat!

Add **er** or **est** when you compare words.

The circus clowns are comparing themselves to one another. Can you help them?

Look at their hats and see how they are different.

See that one hat is **fat**, one is **fatter**, and the other is **fattest**.

Add **er** and **est** to the words that compare things.

My hat is fat.

My hat is fatt<u>er</u>.

My hat is fatt<u>est</u>!

My lollipop is big.

My lollipop is bigg_____.

My lollipop is bigg_____!

1

2

3

I am short.

I am short_____.

I am the short____!

My feet are long.

My feet are long ____.

My feet are the long_____!

Name _____

Comparative Adjectives

Quick Draw

Describing **words** tell how things look, taste, smell, sound, and feel. They also tell how many.

Zilla's drawing book has some pages that need to be finished.

Would you like to finish them?

Read the sentence on each page.

Underline the describing words in each sentence.

Finish drawing each picture and color it.

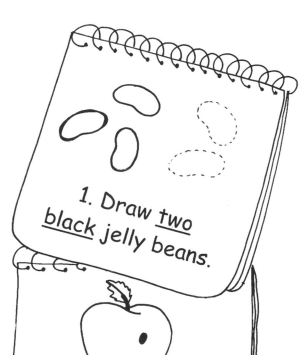

1. Draw <u>two</u> <u>black</u> jelly beans.

4. The green apple has a worm.

2. She has pink polka dots on her shirt.

3. Mrs. Guppy's hat has big, red flowers.

5. What a pretty, happy face!

Name _____

Adjectives

The Clean-Up Crew

A **verb** is an **action** word. Action words tell what people or animals do.

It is late, and the circus show is over.

Not everyone can go to bed, though.

Someone has to clean the big tent and get it ready for tomorrow!

Read the **verbs (action words)** in the dust cloud.

Draw a line from each picture to a verb that tells what that clown is doing.

scrub
sweep   mop
three   sew
carry
wash   paint
pizza

Name _____

Verbs

The Stars of the Show

The circus has many great stars.

Try to match each star to his or her name.

Choose a name that fits each star.

Write the name on the line by the star's picture.

Start each name with a capital letter.

Names are **proper nouns.** They begin with capital letters.

1. _____
   _____

2. _____

3. _____
   _____

4. _____

5. _____

flip	flop
Lolly	honey	berry	strong	sam

Name _____

Proper Nouns

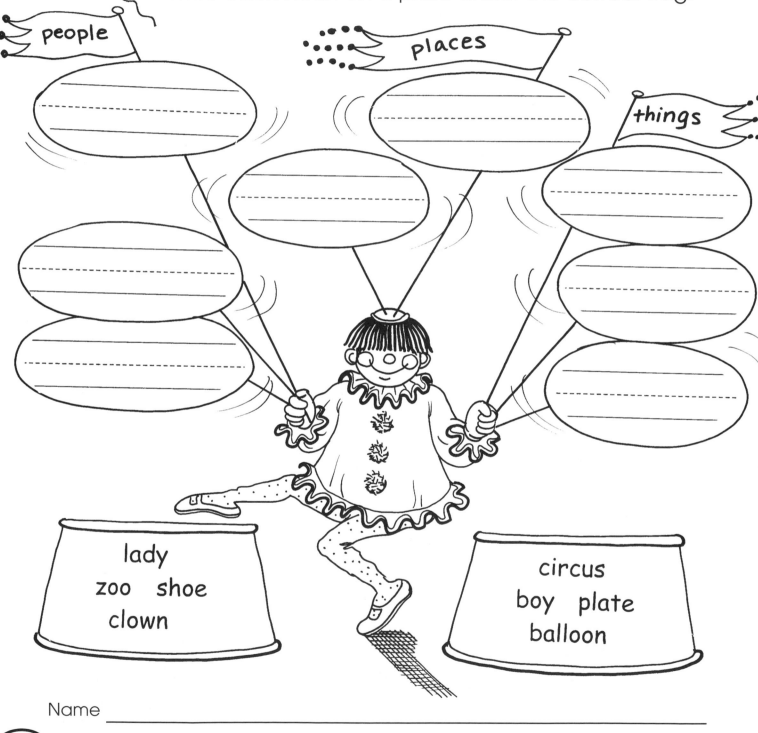

Spinning Plates

A noun is a word that names a person, place, or thing.

How does Lily keep all those plates spinning at the same time? It is amazing that they do not fall! Read the nouns on Lily's stools.

Decide if each noun names a person, place, or thing.

Write each noun on a plate under the correct flag.

people

places

things

lady
zoo shoe
clown

circus
boy plate
balloon

Name _____

Nouns

Run-On Rollo

Rollo, the ringmaster, talks so fast he hardly stops to take a breath!

Read what Rollo is saying, and help him stop between sentences.

Put a period or an exclamation point at the end of each sentence.

Put a capital letter at the beginning of each sentence.

A run-on sentence is two or more sentences that run together.

Step right up! See the oddest show on earth!

look at the pink dinosaur it eats popcorn for dinner

see a kitty as big as a moose and a horse as small as a mouse

I have an ant with two heads there is a dog with six ears

hear my frog sing "Jingle Bells" watch her dance

stare at a snake with arms and legs see a pig fly

watch a flea in pajamas you will not believe your eyes

see a creature from outer space he is goofy

Name _____

Run-On Sentences

All Dressed Up

Wow! These circus folks are all dressed up for the show.
Don't they look good?
Read each group of words in the stars and other shapes.
Color the shape if the words inside make a sentence.

A complete sentence names something and tells what happens.

I work for peanuts.

This hat is too big.

On my head a curly wig.

Ruffles all over.

Funny clowns

We look so cute.

This so small.

Surprise for the show.

Let's have some fun.

I like to dress up.

Stars good on you.

Can you help me?

Name _____

Complete Sentences

Poor Lost Lucky

Bubba lost his little dog, Lucky, at the circus parade.

Color the word blocks that make a sentence in each row below.

Put a capital letter at the beginning and a period at the end of each sentence.

If Bubba follows the path you colored, he will find Lucky!

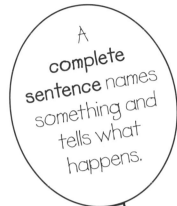

A complete sentence names something and tells what happens.

my	puppy	is	lost	nose	is
see	hug	I	am	so	sad	was
be	I	want	to	find	him	top
parade	he	may	be	hungry	on
gone	help	here	he	is	now

Name _____

Complete Sentences

A Toothless Lion

A complete sentence names something and tells what happens.

The lion used to be the most dangerous animal.

Oh, has he lost his teeth? Give him some new ones.

Each time you find a complete sentence, put a period at the end and draw one tooth in the lion's mouth.

1. In the circus ring

2. A man with a chair

3. The lion is very strong

4. Bars keep the people safe

5. The whip cracks

6. "Rrroar!" says the lion

7. Fire in the circle

8. The strong animal jumps

9. Jump through the hoop

10. A swat of the paw

11. He is an unhappy lion

12. Growling at the lion tamer

13. This is my favorite act

14. He looks grumpy

15. A toothless lion looks funny

How many teeth did you give to the lion?_____

Name _____

Complete Sentences

The Mystery Fizzle

Miss Wizzle keeps a fizzle in her magic pouch.

Here are some sentences about fizzles.

If the sentence asks a question, add a **question mark (?)** to the end.

Then color the star in front of the question.

A **question** is a sentence that asks something. It begins with a capital letter and ends with a ?.

Shhh! He's sleeping.

1. ☆ All fizzles are small

2. ☆ Where do fizzles live

3. ☆ Do fizzles eat pizza

4. ☆ Can you be a fizzle

5. ☆ Are fizzles only in pouches

6. ☆ Fizzles do not like rain

7. ☆ Do you want a fizzle

8. ☆ Fizzles come in many colors

9. ☆ Could a fizzle sing a song

10. ☆ Every fizzle has a friend

What do you think a fizzle Is?

- -

Name _____

Shhh! All Is Quiet!

A *statement* is a sentence that tells something. It begins with a capital letter and ends with a period.

The circus is over for the night. Everyone is sleeping.

Read the sentences in the spaces.

Add a period to each statement. Then color the space yellow.

Color the space blue if the sentence is not a statement.

You will make a nighttime picture!

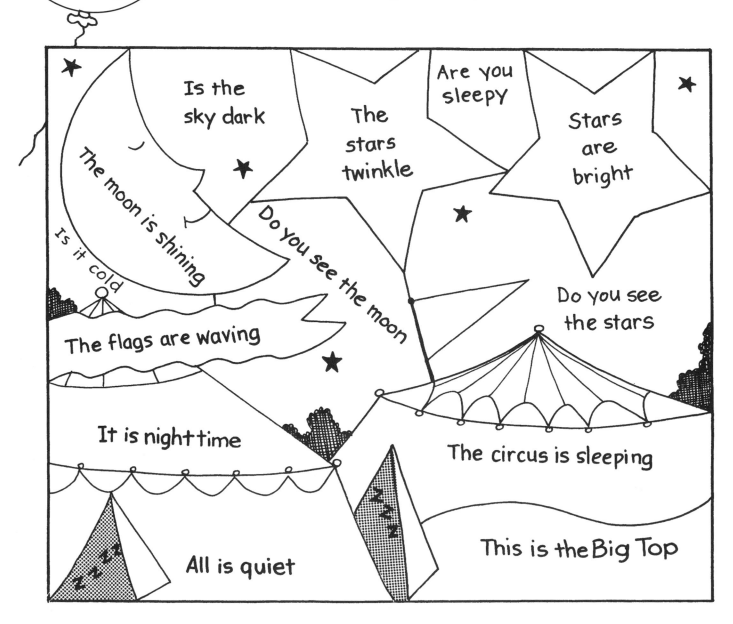

Is the sky dark

Are you sleepy

The stars twinkle

Stars are bright

The moon is shining

Is it cold

Do you see the moon

Do you see the stars

The flags are waving

It is night time

The circus is sleeping

All is quiet

This is the Big Top

Name _____

Statements

Joey the Juggler

Juggling is Joey's favorite thing to do.

Read the words in the balls.

Color the ball yellow if the word is a **verb (an action word).**

Color the other balls red.

A **verb** is a word that shows action, like **play** or **jump.**

boy

big

cat

girl

face

jump

swim

read

sun

juggle

tooth

hat

run

top

hop

ticket

walk

play

black

Name _____

Verbs

Whose Clothes?

Silly clowns! It's time for the show, and they have lost some parts of their costumes.

Trace each name.

Then find the missing part of each clown's costume.

Write that word after the clown's name.

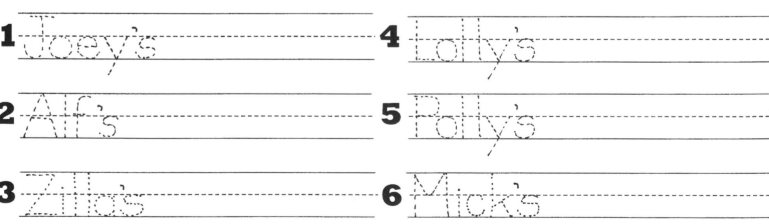

nose   flower   bow   hat   button   glove

1 Joey's

2 Alf's

3 Zilla's

4 Lolly's

5 Polly's

6 Mick's

Name _____

Possessive Nouns

Unpack Your Trunks!

Joey and Zilla are unpacking their trunks.

Joey has one of each thing in his trunk.

Zilla has more than one of everything in her trunk.

Draw a purple line to the things that are Joey's.

Draw a green line to the things that are Zilla's, and add an **s** to each word in her trunk.

Plural means more than one. Add **S** to most nouns to make them plural.

shoe

sock

key

glove

hat

book

pen

shoe ___   sock ___

book ___   glove ___

hat ___   pen ___   key ___

Name _____

Plural Nouns

Zilla's Lost Nose

A *noun* is a word that names a person, place, or thing.

Where, oh where, is Zilla Zucchini's lost nose?

Look for **naming words (nouns)** on the boxes.

If a box has a noun on it, color it green.

Color the other boxes yellow.

You will find a green path right to Zilla's nose!

purple

trunk

silly

flowers

hop

cry

zucchini

circus

nose

shoe

tall

jiggle

lady

tiger

happy

Name _____

The Circus Parade

Here come the animals and the circus acts!

Read the words in the circus parade.

Write an **s** at the end of the word if the picture shows more than one of something.

Color the pictures that show more than one of something.

Plural means more than one. Add **s** to most nouns to make them plural.

elephant____

tiger____

clown____

acrobat____

car____

clown kid____

zebra____

weight lifter____
weight____

fire eater____

seal____

balloon____

tank____

wheel____

bear____

ringmaster____

Name _____

Plural Nouns

The Circus Is Coming!

A **noun** is a word that names a person, place, or thing.

The Apple Pie Circus is coming to town!
Read the words on the circus parade.
Look for **naming words (nouns)**.
If a shape has a naming word, color it red.
Color the other shapes yellow.

Name _____

Nouns

Wild Dreams

Zilla is having a wild and crazy dream.

What do you think it is about?

Write about it here. Tell what you think is happening in Zilla's dream. Draw Zilla's dream in the bubble.

Zilla dreamed about

_____

_____

_____

_____

_____

Name _____

Writing: Imaginative Piece

SOCIAL STUDIES

Skills Exercises
Grade One

SKILLS CHECKLIST
SOCIAL STUDIES

✔	SKILL	PAGE(S)
	Be aware of people, places, and things in the world	130, 131
	Identify characteristics of self; increase self-awareness	132, 133
	Identify ways people grow, learn, and change	134, 135
	Identify important people in your life	136, 137
	Recognize many kinds of families	136, 137
	Identify roles and functions of families	138, 139
	Recognize some different social groups	140
	Identify some rules of societies or families	141
	Read addresses; know your own address	142, 143
	Find information on maps	142, 143, 148, 149, 154–157, 159, 161, 164
	Make a map of your room	144
	Identify places in neighborhoods and communities	145
	Identify different skills that people have	146
	Identify people and jobs in communities	146
	Identify different kinds of transportation	147
	Locate places on a U.S. map	148, 149
	Locate your home on a map of the U.S. and a map of the world	148, 149, 156, 157
	Identify some U.S. symbols, traditions, places, and holidays	150–152
	Identify some famous Americans and their accomplishments	153
	Become familiar with maps of the world; locate continents	154–157
	Explore something about families or cultures throughout the world	154, 155
	Explore the concept of climate	158
	Read a grid map	159
	Examine flags of some nations	160
	Identify N, S, E, W directions	162
	Read information from a simple timeline	163
	Become familiar with some geographic terms and concepts	165

SKILLS CHECKLIST
MAP SKILLS & GEOGRAPHY

✔	SKILL	PAGE(S)
	Define and recognize maps	166, 167
	Identify and use a variety of maps	166–169, 172–177, 180–185
	Use maps to locate things	166, 182–185
	Read and use titles and labels on a map	168, 169, 172–177, 182–185
	Compare locations on a map	168, 174, 180, 182–184
	Identify parts of a map: titles, key, scale, and compass rose	168–177
	Choose titles for maps	169
	Identify and draw map symbols; match symbols to words	170, 171
	Follow compass directions to find things on a map	172–175
	Identify directions on a map (N, S, E, W)	172–175
	Use maps to find information and answer questions	172–177, 180–185
	Use a simple scale to determine distances on a map	176, 177
	Find and place objects on a simple grid	178, 179
	Make a map from a key	179
	Make simple maps	179
	Use map symbols and keys to find things on a map	179, 184, 185
	Locate U.S. on a world map	180, 181
	Recognize continents and oceans on a world map	182, 183

What in the World?

What an adventure!

Layla and Jeff are off on a bike ride with their pets, Biff and Tulip.

They want to explore many places.

They will see many interesting things.

Color the things in the picture that you have seen.

Name _____

Use with page 131.

Environmental Awareness

What in the World? cont.

Color the things that you have seen.

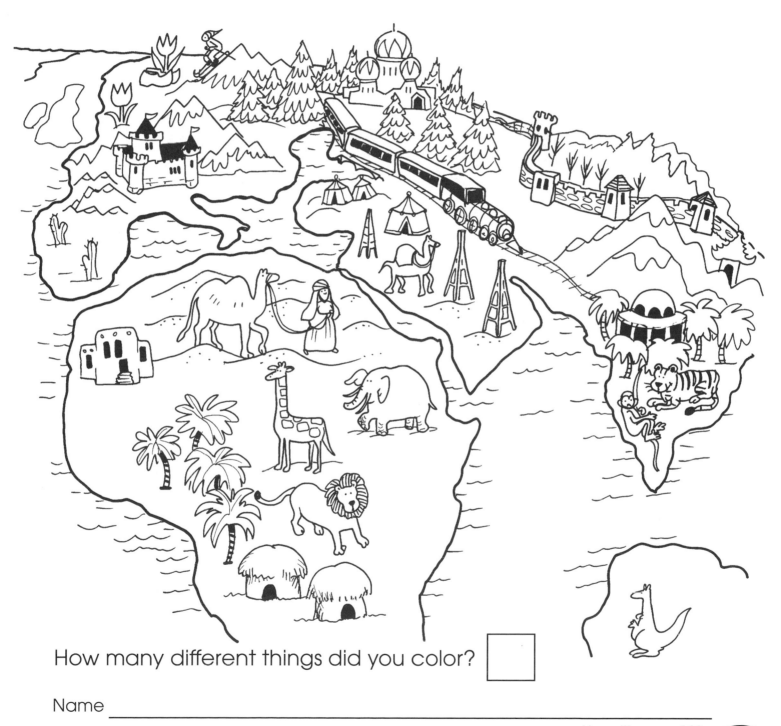

How many different things did you color? ☐

Name _____

Use with page 130.

Environmental Awareness

Meet a VIP!

The letters VIP stand for "Very Important Person."
You are a VIP because no one in the whole world is just like you!
Draw a picture of yourself in the mirror.
Then finish the sentences to tell about you—a VIP!

I really like
_____
- - - - - - - - - - - - - - - - - - -
_____

I do not like
_____
- - - - - - - - - - - - - - - - - - -
_____

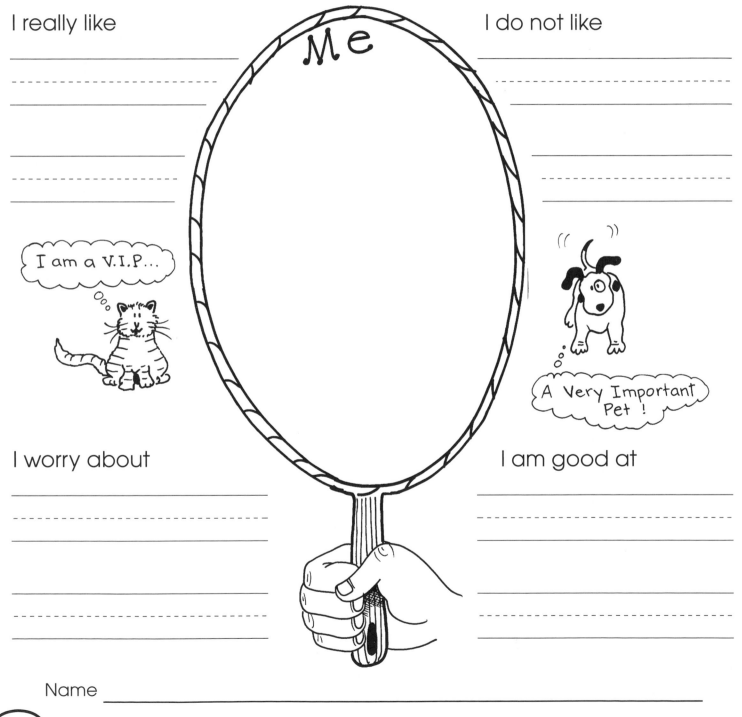

I worry about
_____
- - - - - - - - - - - - - - - - - - -
_____
- - - - - - - - - - - - - - - - - - -

I am good at
_____
- - - - - - - - - - - - - - - - - - -
_____
- - - - - - - - - - - - - - - - - - -

Name _____

Look What You Can Do!

Jeff is really proud of the things his cat Tulip can do.

You can be proud of the many things you can do.

Have you ever thought about how much you can do?
Check (✔)
the things that
you can do.

- [ ] stand on my head
- [ ] play a piano
- [ ] kick a ball
- [ ] write a poem
- [ ] help someone
- [ ] carry a big box
- [ ] climb a tree
- [ ] take care of a baby

- [ ] make some toast
- [ ] tie my shoe
- [ ] clean my room
- [ ] make a phone call
- [ ] use a fire extinguisher
- [ ] wash a car
- [ ] throw a ball
- [ ] feed my pet
- [ ] write a letter
- [ ] read a book
- [ ] make pancakes
- [ ] ride a skateboard

Name _____

Self-Awareness

Once Upon a Time

Everyone was a tiny baby once upon a time.

We don't stay babies for long because we start to grow, learn, and change.

We need to look at pictures to remember how little we were!

Look at Layla's pictures, and see how she has changed.

Write the number of the picture or pictures that show:

1. Layla's parent helping her learn something: ____

2. Layla teaching something to her little brother: ____

3. Layla learning something as a baby: ____

4. Layla learning something all by herself: ____ and ____

Name _____

Growth, Learning, & Change

May be used with page 135.

Yesterday, Today, and Tomorrow

Do you dream about the things you will do when you are a big kid?

Do you remember things you did when you were a little kid?

Look at the pictures of the baby, the child, and the teenager.

Draw something to go along with each picture.

Jeff, age 1

This is something babies can do.

Jeff, age 5

This is something 5-year-olds can do.

Jeff, age 15

This is something teenagers can do.

Name _____

May be used with page 134.

Growth, Learning, & Change

All Shapes and Sizes

People come in different shapes, colors, and sizes.
Do you know what? So do families!
Each family is different and special.
Count the number of people in each different family.
Then draw a picture of your own family.

Name _____

Use with page 137.

Families

All Shapes and Sizes, cont.

F ☐

G ☐

H ☐

I ☐

Draw your own family here!

Name _____

Use with page 136.

Families

Big Helping Hands

Layla's family and your family are like families all over the world.

People in families try to help each other.

What are some of the ways the big people in your family help you?

Write five ways on the big hand.

Can you write on the fingers?

Name _____

May be used with page 139.

Roles & Functions in Families

Little Helping Hands

Small people help families, too!
Trace around your own hand on this page.
Write some things you do to help your family.
Write on the hand or fingers.

Name _____

May be used with page 138.

Roles & Functions in Families

The Growing Garden

The world is like a big garden with paths that lead to many places and groups where you can grow and learn.

The path begins in your home with your family.
It goes to other places or groups where you grow and learn.
Some of these groups and places are named in the box.
Write the number of the picture next to the matching word.

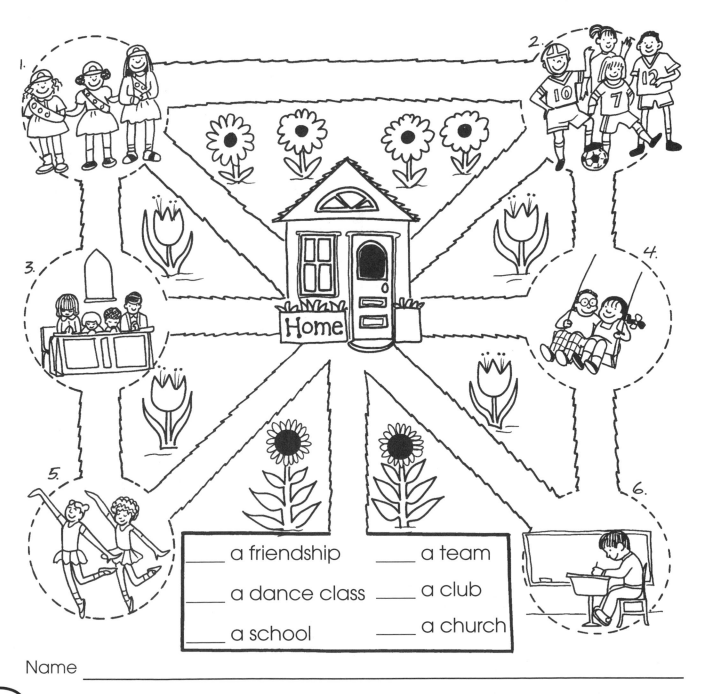

_____ a friendship   _____ a team

_____ a dance class   _____ a club

_____ a school   _____ a church

Name _____

Social Groups

What Are Rules For?

What do you think it would be like if there were no rules?
Maybe you could stay up all night or eat all day!

Rules have reasons: They keep people safe and healthy.
They also help people get along.

Write the number of the picture that shows the answer.

1. Which picture shows a rule to keep someone healthy? ____
2. Which picture shows a rule to keep someone safe? ____
3. Which picture shows a rule about sharing? ____
4. Color the picture that shows someone not following a rule.

Name _____

Rules of Social Groups

Cookie Delivery

Layla is a Girl Scout.

She is delivering cookies to her neighbors.

Help her and her mom find the right addresses.

> The number of a house and the name of a street make up an address.

Use the map on this page and on page 143.

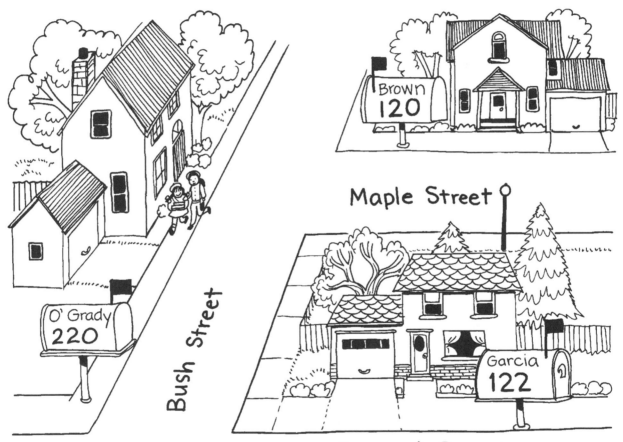

Circle the right answer.

1. Layla likes to pet the O'Gradys' cat. What is their address?

    124 Maple Street   220 Maple Street   220 Bush Street

2. Who lives at 126 Second Street?

    The Adams   The Steins   The Browns

Name _____

Read Addresses

3. Which families share a house on Second Street?

The Chens and the Adams

The Browns and the Chens   The Travises and the Habeebs

4. Who lives next door to the Garcias?

The Habeebs   The Steins   The Adams

Maple Street

Second Street

5. What street does Layla cross to get from the Browns' to the Garcias'?

Bush Street   Maple Street   Second Street

6. What is the Chens' address?

120 Maple Street   124 Second Street   124 Maple Street

Name _____

Use with page 142.

Read Addresses

Just the Way You Want It

Layla wants to change her room around.

She is making a map of the way she wants her room to be.

Have you ever wanted to change your room?

Draw a map of your room with everything the way you want it!

Name _____

Make a Map

Where Should He Go?

When Jeff wants to read a good book, he goes to his town library.
The library is on the map in row B and row 4. It is at B, 4.
Where should Jeff go to do the things below?
Give the location on the map for each answer.
Where should he go to . . .

1. . . . buy groceries? **A, 1**

2. . . . save money? ____

3. . . . play on a swing? ____

4. . . . see a doctor? ____

5. . . . eat a hamburger? ____

6. . . . buy shoes? ____

7. . . . get gas? ____

8. . . . buy fresh bread? ____

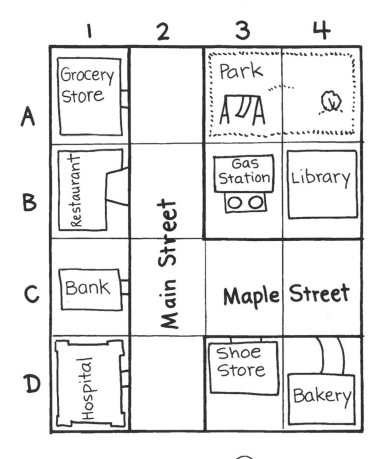

Name _____

Neighborhood Places

Workers Everywhere You Look!

Wow! What a busy bustling city!

On their bus ride across the city, Layla and Jeff see many people working at different jobs!

Circle as many different workers as you can find.

Color the ones who are doing something you might like to do.

How many workers did you find? _____

Name _____

Workers in the Community

Coming and Going

Jeff and Layla get around on their bicycle.

People get around lots of other ways, too.

They can drive, float, fly, skate, sail, walk, or take a train!

Color all the kinds of transportation that you have used.

Draw a circle around your favorite kind of transportation.

Name _____

Transportation

Which Is Yours?

Jeff and his family took a trip across the United States.

Can you find his family?

Use a red crayon to trace Jeff's route.

Read the names of all the states and territories he and his family traveled through.

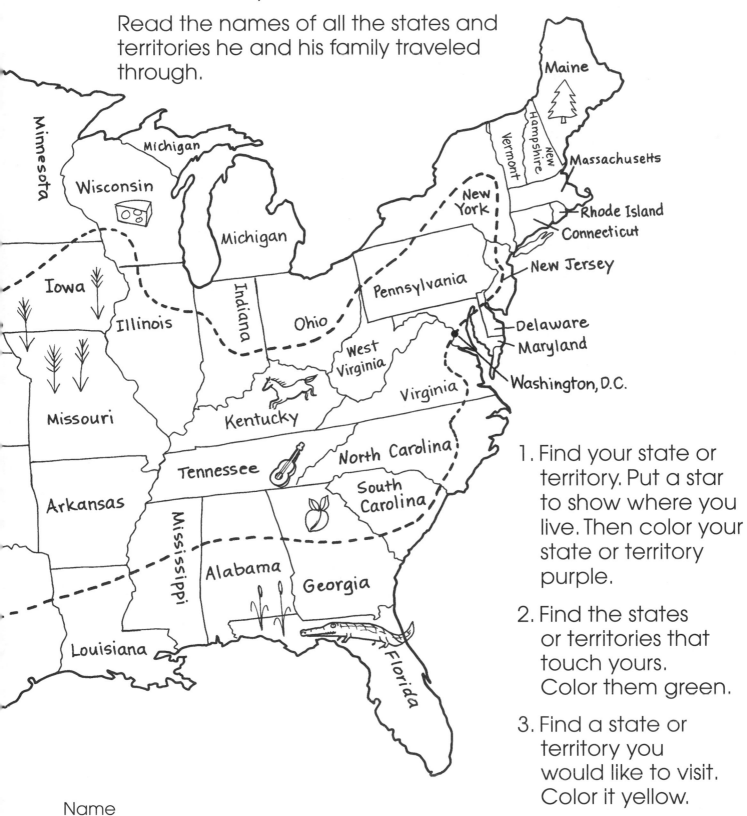

1. Find your state or territory. Put a star to show where you live. Then color your state or territory purple.

2. Find the states or territories that touch yours. Color them green.

3. Find a state or territory you would like to visit. Color it yellow.

Name _____

Use with page 148.

Read a U.S. Map

The American Parade

The kids are marching in a big parade to celebrate the United States.

The parade is full of American symbols.

Symbols are special pictures or things that stand for something about the country.

Look for all the symbols listed below. Color each one as you find it.

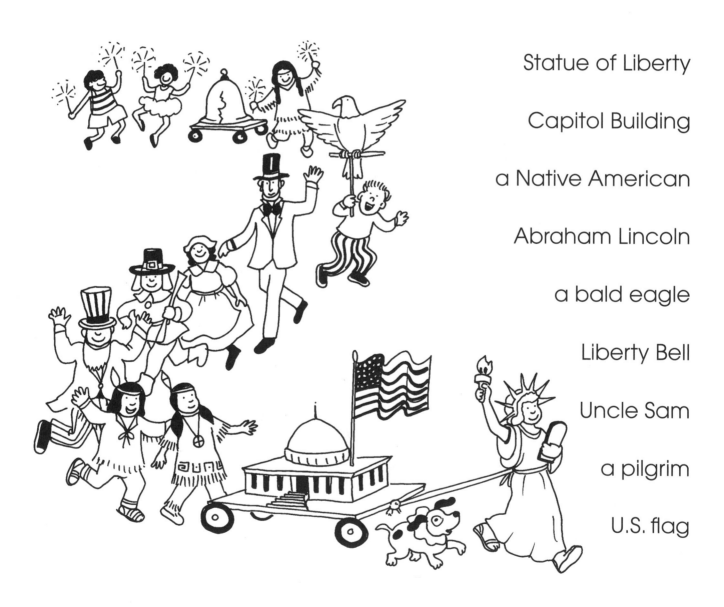

Statue of Liberty

Capitol Building

a Native American

Abraham Lincoln

a bald eagle

Liberty Bell

Uncle Sam

a pilgrim

U.S. flag

Name _____

U.S. Symbols & Traditions

A Very Famous House

It's the most famous house in the United States!
The address is 1600 Pennsylvania Avenue in Washington, D.C.
Connect the dots, and you will make a picture of this great house!

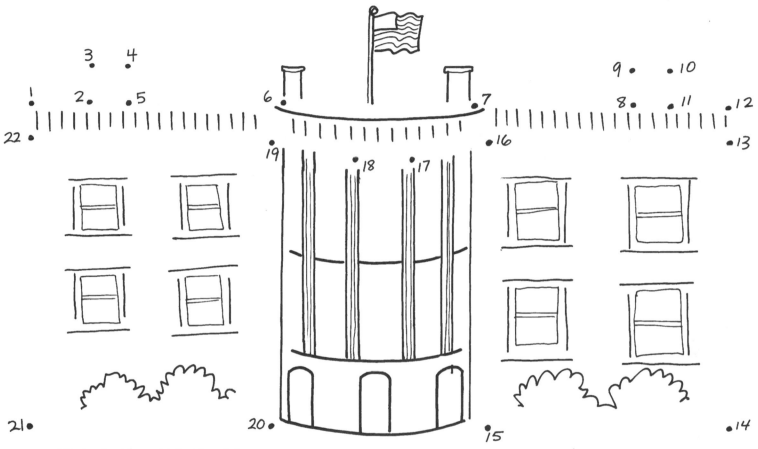

This is the White House.

It has 132 rooms and 35 bathrooms.

It is the home for the president of the United States
and the president's family.

The president's office is in a part of the White House.

What is the name of the president who lives there today?

_____

- -

Name _____

American Places

A Very Famous Bird

The American bald eagle is a symbol of the United States. It is the most famous bird in America!

Connect the dots to see what this eagle looks like!

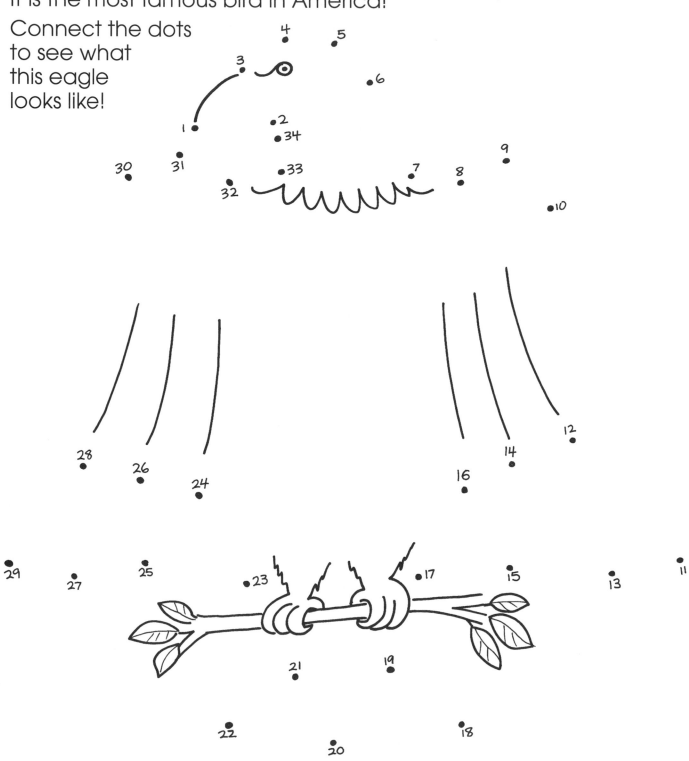

Name _____

American Symbols

Some Very Famous People

Jeff loves the museum.

It is full of all kinds of interesting things from the past.

Today he is looking at pictures of some important Americans.

Write the number from each picture next to the matching name.

Museum Guide

1.

2.

3.

Martin Luther King, Jr.
A leader who helped get fair treatment for black Americans

Abraham Lincoln
American president who helped free the slaves

Betsy Ross
Woman who probably made the first U.S. flag

Sally Ride
America's first female astronaut to travel in space

George Washington
America's first president

4.

5.

Name _____

Everyone Is from Somewhere!

These kids live in homes all over the world.

Which one is from which continent?

Each kid has a clue to tell you
which continent is home.

Draw a line from each kid to the
right spot for his or her home.

Layla lives in the
United States on
the continent of
North America.

Roberto is from Brazil
on the continent of
South America.

Name _____

Use with page 155.

Read a World Map

Everyone Is from Somewhere! cont.

Draw a line from each kid to the right spot for his or her home.

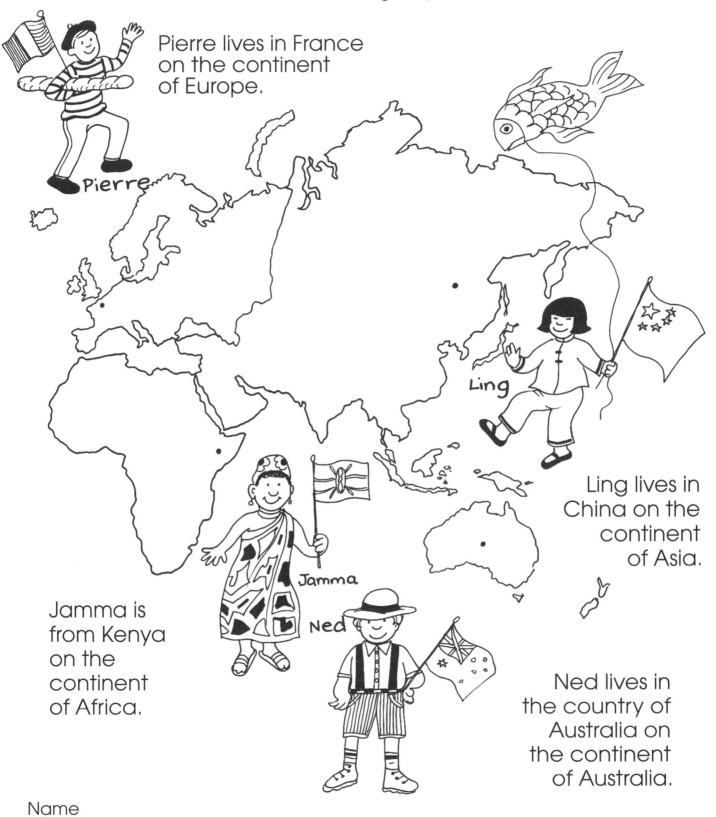

Pierre lives in France on the continent of Europe.

Ling lives in China on the continent of Asia.

Jamma is from Kenya on the continent of Africa.

Ned lives in the country of Australia on the continent of Australia.

Name _____

Where in the World Are You?

What if the mail carrier wants to deliver a letter to you, but does not have your address. Where in the world are you?

Give the mail carrier a little help in finding you.

Write your address on the mailbox, and draw your house.

Draw your house here.

_____
Your Name

_____
Your Street

_____
Your City

_____
Your State / Territory / Province

If you live in the continental United States, color your state at the right. If not, write the name of your state, territory, or province below.

_____

Put a star to show where your town or city is in the state on the outline map.

Name _____

Use with page 157.

Locate Home

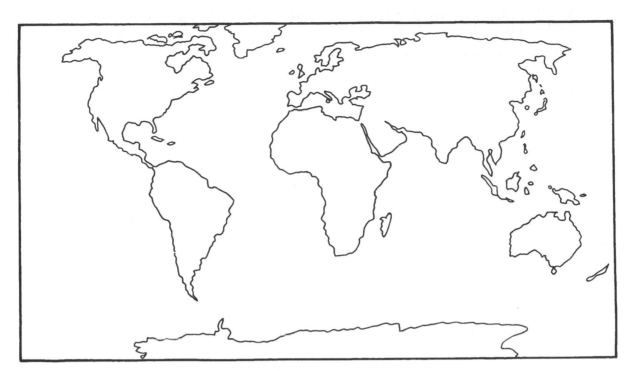

Color the continent that you live on.

Write the name of
your country here. _____

Write the name of
your continent here. _____

Find your planet. Circle it.

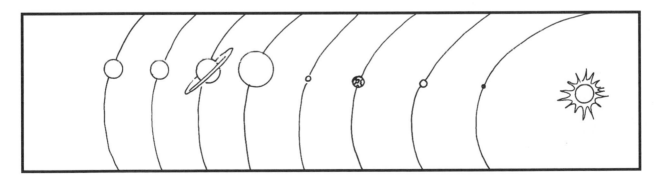

Write the name of
your planet here. _____

Name _____

Locate Home

Some Like It Hot! Some Like It Cold!

These four travelers are all dressed for different climates.
Help them find the right place to go.
Draw a path from each one to the climate that is the right match!

Name _____

Climate

Which Square?

Two friends are taking a rest on the bench in the park.
Which square are they sitting in?
The square is in row A and row 2. They are in square A, 2!
Find some other things on the park map!

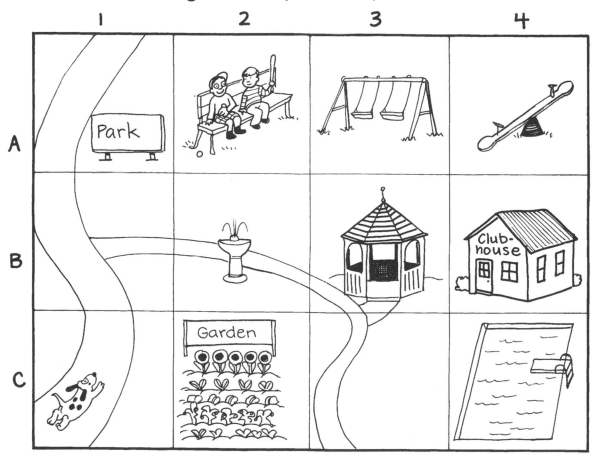

1. Where is the ? _____   5. Where is the  ? _____

2. Where is the ? _____   6. Where is the ? _____

3. Where is the ? _____   7. Where is the ⟨Park⟩ ? _____

4. Color the thing in C, 2 green.   8. Color the building in B, 4 red.

Name _____

Read a Grid Map

Great Flags!

Every country has a flag!

They are all different and beautiful.

In art class, Jeff and Layla are drawing flags of some different countries around the world.

Help them color these flags from four different countries.

Argentina

Light Blue

White

Light Blue

Canada

Red

White

Red

Red

Philippines

Dark Blue

Yellow

White

Red

United States

Blue Background

Red
White
Red
White
Red
White
Red

White
Red
White
Red
White
Red

Name _____

Flags of Nations

Where Is Tulip?

Tulip the cat was at home with Jeff just a few minutes ago.

Now she is lost somewhere in the neighborhood!

Will Jeff find her?

Draw Jeff's trail on the map and find out!

1. Jeff leaves his apartment.

2. He looks behind Sam's house.

3. He walks south on Maple Street.

4. He looks around the swimming pool.

5. He looks under the slide.

6. He looks behind the school.

7. He looks in Layla's tree.

8. He looks in Maria's yard.

9. He looks in the sandbox.

10. He finds Tulip at the top of the flagpole!

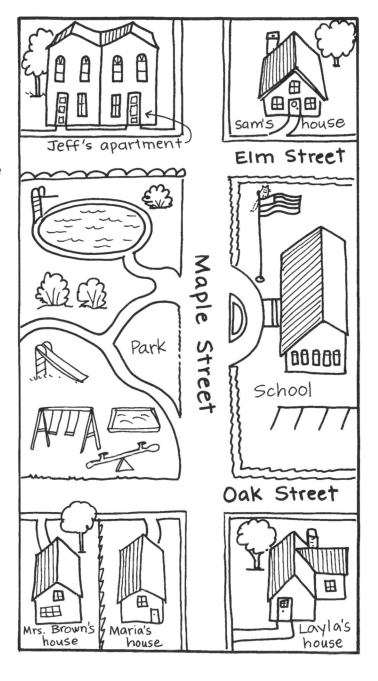

Name _____

Read a Map

Never Eat Squiggly Worms!

This silly sentence is a good one for you to remember. It helps you remember the directions on the Earth and on maps. The first letter of each word stands for the first letter of the direction:

N—NORTH   E—EAST   S—SOUTH   W—WEST

Layla is using her arms and legs to show the directions.

1. Write the correct direction in each space.
2. The sun rises in the east in the morning.
   Draw a bright yellow sun on the east side of the paper.
3. The sun sets in the west in the evening.
   Draw a red sunset on the west side of the paper.

Name _____

Directions on a Map

Time to Celebrate!

Everybody loves a celebration! Jeff's timeline shows some events he has celebrated in his life. Read the timeline to answer the questions.

1. What year did Jeff move to a new house? _____

2. What birthday did he celebrate in 2013? _____

3. What year did Jeff get his kitten? _____

4. What year did he learn to walk? _____

5. What year was his 4th birthday? _____

6. What year did he start school? _____

2010
Born, January 2
First tooth, May

2011
First step
First word

2012
Moved to new house

2013
Third birthday
New kitten named Tulip

2014
Fourth birthday
Learned to ride a bike

2015
First day of school September 10th
Got glasses

2016
Sixth birthday
First grade
New baby sister

Name _____

Read a Timeline

Looking for Biff

Jeff and Layla are off on their bicycle looking for another lost pet!
Follow the paw prints with Jeff and Layla to find Biff the dog.
Then answer the questions, and follow the directions.

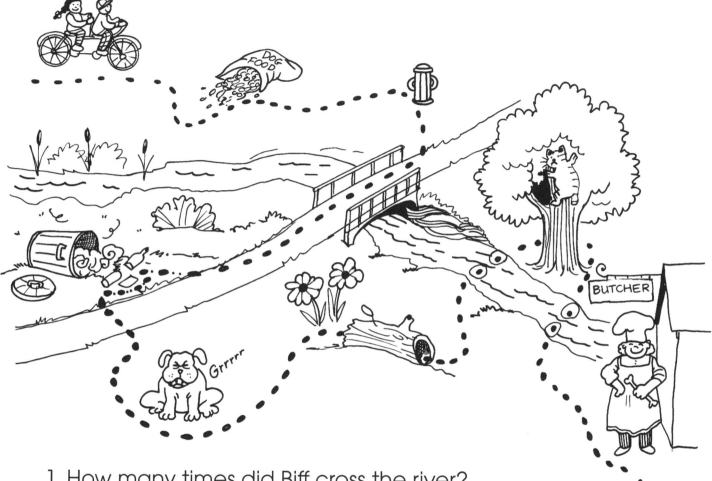

1. How many times did Biff cross the river?_____
2. Color the fire hydrant red.
3. Find the thing Biff crawled through. Color it brown.
4. Find the cat in the tree. Draw a tail on her.
5. Color the garbage can green.
6. Color the friend who gave Biff a snack.
7. Color the unfriendly dog brown.
8. Find Biff, and color the house he is in!

Name _____

Puzzled by Geography

These good friends are doing a geography puzzle.

They are getting a little help from Tulip the cat.

They need your help, too.

Look at the picture clues, and then find the answers in the **Word Box**.

CLUES

Down

1.

2.

3.

Across

4.

5.

6.

7.

WORD BOX

bay
island
volcano
mountain
globe
ocean
trees

Name _____

Noah's Neighborhood

Noah took a ride in a hot air balloon.

He looked down at his neighborhood from the sky.

He drew a pretty good map.

Color the map that Noah drew.

Color Noah's house red.

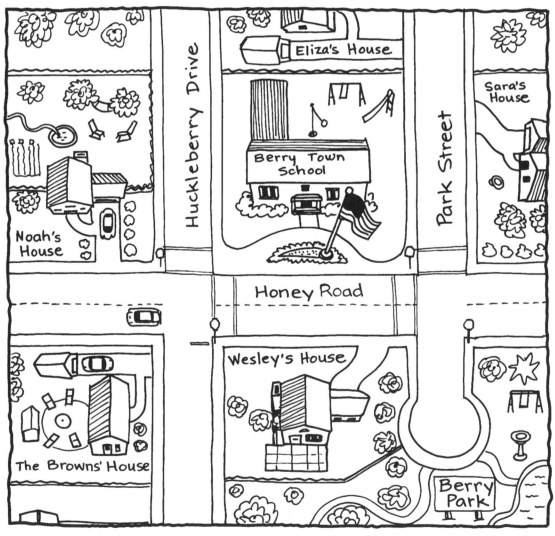

A **map** is a drawing that represents an area.

Name _____

Define & Recognize Maps

His Own Backyard

Noah's hot air balloon landed in his own backyard.

He drew three maps of his yard.

Only one map is correct.

Color the one that is the correct map of his backyard.

A **map** is a drawing that represents an area.

1.

2.

3.

Name _____

Define & Recognize Maps

Moving Day

Grandma and Grandpa Bear are moving to the country.

The map will help them find their new home.

Read about the parts of the map.

Draw a line from each **bold** word to the correct part on the map.

1. The **title** tells what the map is about.
2. The **key** tells what the pictures mean.
3. The **scale** tells about distances.
4. The **compass rose** shows directions.

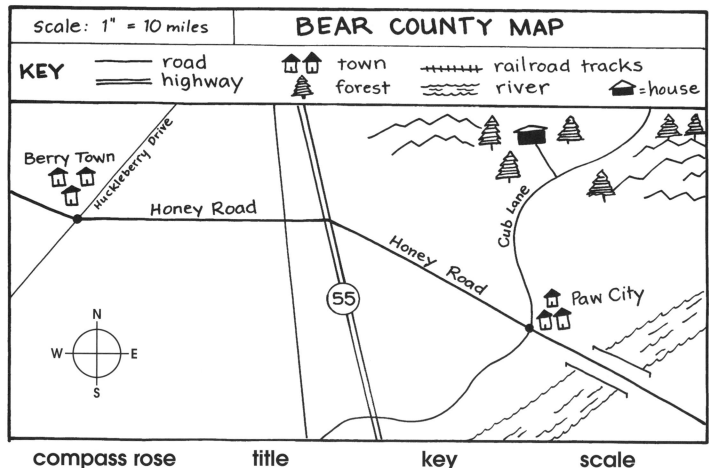

| Scale: 1" = 10 miles | BEAR COUNTY MAP |

KEY —— road ⌂⌂ town ┼┼┼┼ railroad tracks
═══ highway 🌲 forest ≈≈≈ river ⌂=house

Berry Town
Huckleberry Drive
Honey Road
55
Honey Road
Cub Lane
Paw City

N
W ✦ E
S

compass rose   title   key   scale

Name _____

Parts of a Map

The Lost Titles

Grandpa Bear is going to buy peanuts to make a peanut butter pie.

Oops! The wind blew all the titles off his new maps.

Draw a line from each map to the right title.

1.

Honey Road

Fish Lake

Camp Fishy

Bear River

Country Shopping Center

2.

FISH MARKET

Yarn Shop

Grocery Store

Peanut Store

Center Rd.

Cub Lane

Fish Lake Campground

Berry Town Airport

3.

TICKETS

HANGAR

RUNWAY

TOWER

Which map will help Grandpa find the store?   **1   2   3**

Name _____

Map Titles

Maxie Makes Maps

Maxie is a mapmaker.

She draws the symbols that show things on maps.

Draw a line from each symbol to the word that tells what it means.

> The pictures on a map are called **symbols.**

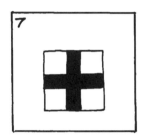

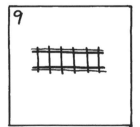

town   railroad

hospital   school

playground   trees

picnic area fire station

campground

Draw some symbols on the next page (page 171).

Name _____

Map Symbols

Use with page 171.

Maxie Makes Maps, cont.

Poor Maxie is worn out from drawing maps.

She needs your help.

Draw a map symbol to match each word.

forest

airport

road

lake

mountains

house

river

Name _____

Use with page 170.

Map Symbols

Follow the Paw Prints

Benjy and his mother walked to the beach.

Benjy stopped to pick berries, but his mother kept walking.

Help Benjy follow the right paw prints to find his way.

Color Mother Bear's paw print path purple.

Follow the directions.

1. Go 3 steps south.

2. Go 4 steps east.

3. Go 4 steps south.

4. Go 4 steps west.

5. Go 3 steps south.

6. Go 3 steps east.

7. Go 2 steps south.

Name _____

Directions

Crab Walk

While Benjy sleeps, a little crab tries to find his way to the ocean.

Look at all the stuff he has to go around!

Read the directions, and draw a path for the crab.

1. Go south to the picnic basket.

2. Go west to the beach ball.

3. Go south to the straw hat.

4. Go east to the flipper.

5. Go north to the umbrella.

6. Go east to Benjy.

7. Go south into the ocean.

Name _____

Which Birdhouse?

Sara Bearheart has valentines for her bird friends.

She can't remember which house belongs to which bird!

Help her find the right house for each valentine.

Draw a line from each valentine to the right house.

Jay's house is farthest north.

Robin lives east of the birdbath.

Canary lives west of the birdbath.

Blackbird lives south of Canary.

Sparrow lives south of the birdbath.

Name _____

Find the Berry Pie

Sara and Wesley smell something wonderful!

They climb the wall looking for the hot berry pie they smell.

Read the two boxes to find the paths they climb.

Color a green path for Sara.

Color a red path for Wesley.

Sara ↑   Wesley ↑

Sara climbs . . .	Wesley climbs . . .
4 bricks N	2 bricks N
2 bricks E	brick E
1 brick S	1 brick S
1 brick E	1 brick E
4 bricks N	6 bricks N
2 bricks W	brick W

Name _____

Peek Into the Dollhouse

Eliza Bear wants to put rugs in her dollhouse.
Help her measure the rooms and the hall!

Use your thumb to measure.

On this map, 1 thumb equals
1 foot in the dollhouse.

A **scale** shows
distance on a map.

Living Room

Baby
Doll's
Room

Big
Doll's
Room

upstairs

Hall

Hall

Hall

Kitchen

Bathroom

Use your thumb to measure.

1. How long are the stairs?
_____ feet

2. How long is the baby's
bedroom? _____ feet

3. How long is the living
room? _____ feet

4. How long is the kitchen?
_____ feet

5. How long is the hallway by
the bedrooms? _____ feet

Name _____

Visit to the Candy Store

Uncle Beanie delivers candy to the candy store.
He wonders if his big box will fit in the door!
Look at the ruler by the door to see how wide the door is.
Look at the other rulers to see other distances.

Candy Store Scale 1 inch = 1 foot

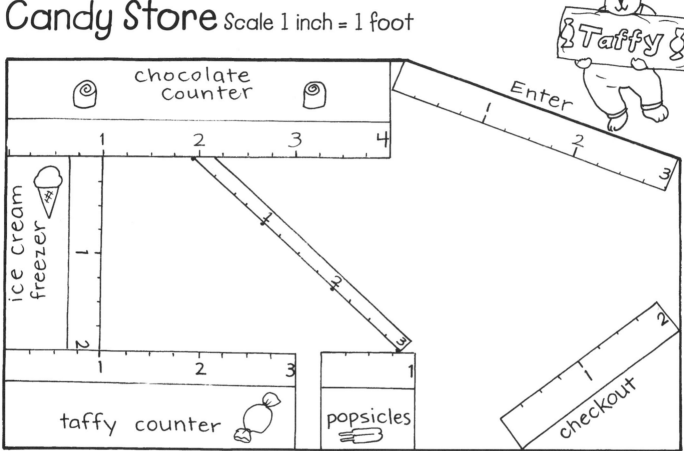

Answer the questions.

1. Beanie's box is $1\frac{1}{2}$ feet wide. Will it fit through the door? **yes   no**

2. How long is the checkout? _____ feet

3. How long is the taffy counter? _____ feet

4. How long is the ice cream freezer? _____ feet

5. How long is the chocolate counter? _____ feet

6. How far is it from the chocolates to the popsicles? _____ feet

Name _____

A Bear-y Fine Picnic

It is a sunny day for the Bear family picnic!
Everyone brought some yummy food.
Look where they put things on the blanket.
Draw more food for them to eat. Follow the directions.

The banana is in E, 3 on the grid.

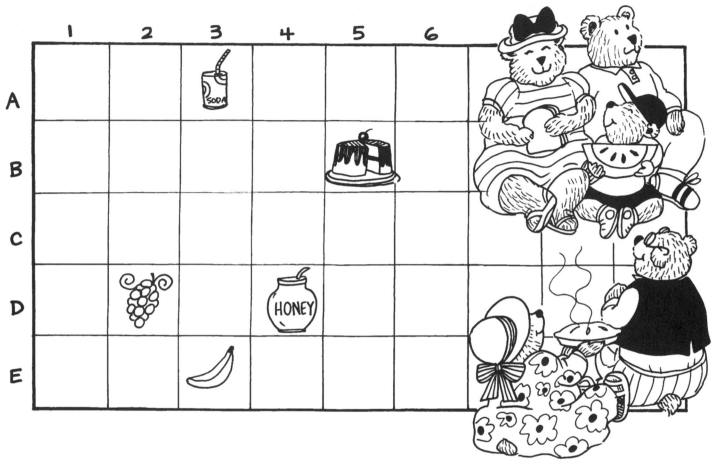

1. Draw a  in C, 1.

2. Draw an in C, 3.

3. Draw a in B, 4.

4. Draw an in A, 1.

5. Where is the  ? _____

6. Where are the 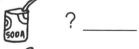 ? _____

7. Where is the  ? _____

8. Where is the ? _____

Name _____

Find & Place Things on a Grid

A Pizza Map

Grandpa Bear wanted to bring pizza to the picnic.

Draw a map of the pizza Grandpa made.

Use the symbols from the **map key.**

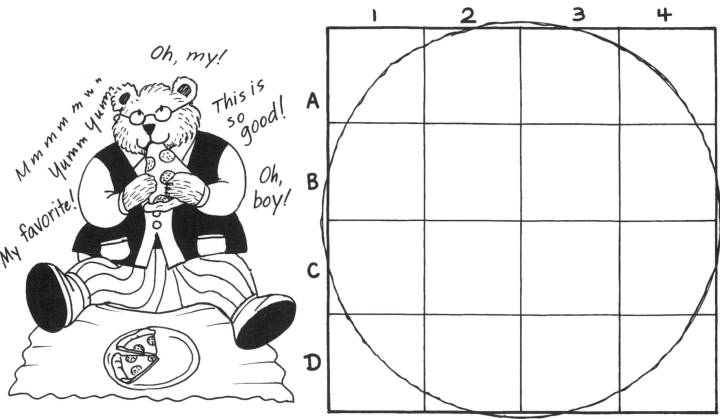

Follow the directions:

1. Draw olives in A, 4; D, 1; and D, 3.

2. Draw pepperoni in A, 2; B, 1; B, 3; C, 3; and D, 2.

3. Draw mushrooms in A, 3; B, 2; and C, 1.

4. Draw pineapple in B, 4; C, 2; C, 4; and D, 4.

Name _____

Place Things on a Grid

Where in the Universe?

There is a delivery for Benjy from outer space! Where is he?
Follow the directions to show his address in the universe.

Benjy Bearclaw
10 Honey Road
Berry Town, Wisconsin
U.S.A.
North America
Planet Earth

1. Color Benjy's planet.

2. Color Benjy's continent.

THE WORLD MAP

Name _____

Locate U.S. Address

Where in the Universe? cont.

3. Color Benjy's country.

4. Color Benjy's state.

5. Draw a picture of Benjy's home.

Name _____

Use with page 180.

Locate U.S. Address

Where in the World?

Where in the world is Miss Grizz going on this big ship?

Use a red crayon to trace the dotted path her ship will take.

Follow these directions.

1. Color North America green.
2. Color South America orange.
3. Color Europe red.
4. Color Asia yellow.
5. Color Africa brown.
6. Color Antarctica pink.
7. Color Australia purple.

Pacific Ocean

NORTH AMERICA

Atlantic Ocean

SOUTH AMERICA

Name _____

Use with page 183.

Continents & Oceans

Where in the World? cont.

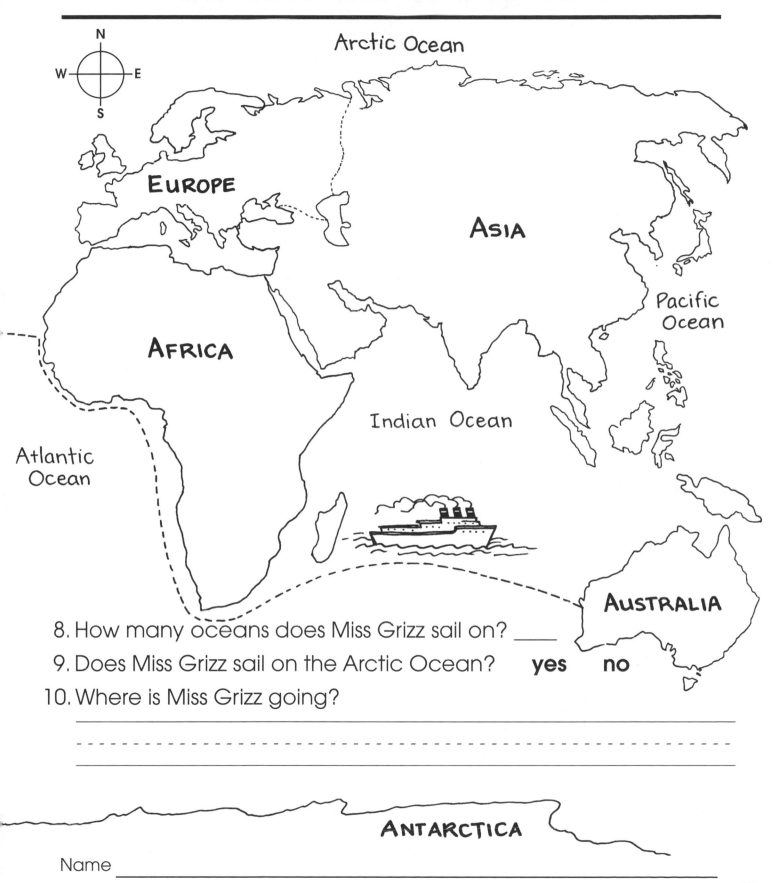

Arctic Ocean

EUROPE

ASIA

Pacific Ocean

AFRICA

Indian Ocean

Atlantic Ocean

AUSTRALIA

ANTARCTICA

8. How many oceans does Miss Grizz sail on? _____

9. Does Miss Grizz sail on the Arctic Ocean?   **yes   no**

10. Where is Miss Grizz going?

_____

- -

_____

Name _____

Use with page 182.

Continents & Oceans

The Trash Collector

Get out the trash cans!

Here comes George to collect the trash!

Read about George's route for picking up trash.

Draw the route George follows on the map. Use a red crayon.

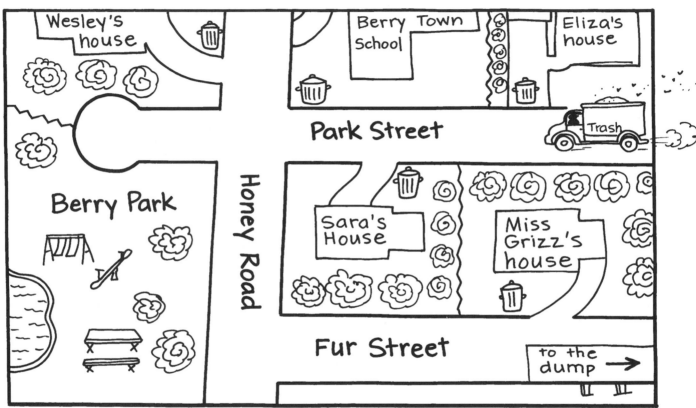

1. He picks up Eliza's trash.

2. Then he picks up Sara's trash.

3. Then he gets trash at Berry Town School.

4. Then he gets Wesley's trash.

5. Then he goes to Miss Grizz's house.

6. At last, he heads for the dump!

Name _____

Find Information on a Map

Which Desk Is Which?

Benjy got to school early.

What is he going to do before class?

Read about what Benjy does, and draw a path for him. Use a red crayon.

1. Benjy stops at the closet to hang up his coat.

2. He goes to the sink to wash his hands.

3. He visits Miss Grizz to say, "Hello!"

4. He puts his books on his desk. It is the third desk in Row 2.

5. He visits the snakes in the snake tank.

6. Then he goes to the art table to paint a picture.

Name _____

Find Information on a Map

SCIENCE

Skills Exercises
Grade One

SKILLS CHECKLIST
SCIENCE

✔	SKILL	PAGE(S)
	Distinguish between living and nonliving things	189–191
	Identify some parts of plants	192
	Recognize the life cycle of plants	193
	Identify some animal groups and their characteristics	194–196
	Describe some animal coverings	197
	Describe some animal movements	198
	Identify animal tracks	199
	Describe ways animals protect themselves	200
	Identify some animal homes	201
	Identify some animal habitats	202, 203
	Identify and describe the body's senses	204, 205
	Recognize healthy foods	206
	Identify and describe some ways to take care of your health	206–208
	Identify some safety behaviors and skills	209
	Identify characteristics of seasons	210, 211
	Identify and describe the three states of matter	212, 213
	Distinguish between solids, liquids, and gases	212, 213
	Describe and define some changes in matter	214
	Identify some properties of air	215, 216
	Identify some properties of water	217
	Identify some causes of pollution	218
	Describe kinds of precipitation and weather conditions	219
	Identify some pushing and pulling forces	220, 221
	Describe some properties of magnets	221
	Identify some uses of electricity	222

Is It Alive?

Here are 7 things that are true of living things.

1. They use food.
2. They grow.
3. They breathe air or take in gases.
4. They move.
5. They respond to things around them.
6. They give off wastes.
7. They make other living things like themselves.

Follow the directions below each picture. Then color the picture.

Am I alive? How can you tell?

4. Draw the sun.

1. Draw a leaf for the caterpillar to eat.

5. Draw a vine for the monkey to swing on.

2. Draw a small turtle.

6. Draw a litter box.

 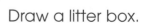

3. Draw air bubbles.

7. Draw some eggs under the hen.

Name _____

Life Characteristics

Alive?

Meg and her pet, Rufus Rat, see living things all around them.

Plants and animals are living things. So are humans!

Living things need air, water, and food.

Living things make more things like themselves.

Color the things on this page that are alive.

Name _____

Use with page 191.

Life Characteristics

Not Alive!

All living things need air, water, and food.

Living things grow.

Some of these things are not alive.

Color the things on this page that are not alive.

Name _____

What Good Are Plant Parts?

Meg's garden is full of plants.

Plants are living things.

Plants eat, drink, and breathe to stay alive.

Follow the directions to learn about the parts of a plant.

Leaves
help a plant make food.
Color the leaves light green.

Stems
hold up the leaves
and flowers.
Color the stems dark green.

Roots
hold the plants in the ground
and drink in water for the plant.
Color all the plant roots brown.

Flowers
make seeds.
The seeds grow new plants.
Color the flowers
any colors you like!

Name _____

Which Happened First?

Look at all the seeds Meg has planted in little plastic cups!

These seeds will grow into plants with leaves and flowers.

The flowers will make new seeds.

Then the plants will shrink and die and drop the seeds.

The seeds will grow into new plants!

This is called a **life cycle.**

Number the pictures in the
order of the plant life cycle.

Name _____

Bugs in the Flower Bed

Rufus Rat thinks there are too many bugs in the garden.

Some of these bugs are insects and some are other kinds of bugs. **Insects** have 6 legs and 2 feelers.

Color the bugs in the garden that are insects.

Name _____

Animal Classification

Going Buggy!

The bugs on the flowers are missing their legs!

They need you to draw legs for them.

The bugs with feelers are **insects.** Insects have 6 legs.

The rest of the bugs are **spiders.** Draw 8 legs on the spiders.

Name _____

Animal Classification

Mixed-Up Zoo

Oh, no! Some of the zoo animals are in the wrong places!

Each zoo area has one or two animals that do not belong there.

Help Meg find these animals and get them with the right group.

Color each animal that is in the wrong place.

Draw a path for the animal back to the place where it belongs.

Name _____

Animal Classification

What Do Animals Wear?

Animals usually do not wear clothes.

Fur, feathers, shells, and scales are special coverings that animals wear instead of clothes.

There are different kinds of animal coverings.

1. Draw a green circle around the animal that wears scales.

2. Draw a red circle around the animal that wears a shell.

3. Draw a yellow circle around the animal that wears smooth, wet skin.

4. Color the animal that wears feathers.

5. Draw a blue circle around the animal that wears fur.

6. Draw a purple circle around the animal that wears hair and clothes.

Name _____

Animals on the Move

How does Meg's pony move? Does it . . .

run?   hop?   swim?   crawl?   fly?   walk?   climb?

Meg sees many different animals on her ride.

Each animal moves in a different way.

Write the word that tells how each animal moves.

1. _____

2. _____

3. _____

4. _____

5. _____

6. _____

Name _____

Animal Movements

Animal Footprints

Animals and people leave footprints where they step.

These are called **tracks.**

Each kind of animal has a different track.

Draw a line to match the tracks with the right animals.

Hint: One animal is dragging its tail!

Name _____

Danger!

Rufus has a trick to try to keep away from danger.

Other animals have ways to keep safe, too.

Match the words to the pictures of ways animals protect themselves.

Draw lines from the words to the pictures of the animals protecting themselves.

Where did that little rat go?

1.

hide
run away
sting
make noise
warn

3.

2.

4.

5.

Draw a picture of
an animal running away.

Name _____

Animal Protection

Something Is Wrong!

Meg has a great book of animal stickers.

Her silly pet, Rufus Rat, stuck most of the stickers on the wrong homes.

Color the animal that is in the right home.

Draw a line from the other animals to their real homes.

Animal Stickers

FIDO

Name _____

A Place to Belong

Every animal lives in a place with other plants and animals.
This is called a **habitat.**

There are many different kinds of habitats all over the world.

Help Meg figure out which habitat is right for the animals she drew.

Draw each of her animals into the right habitat on the next page.

Meg's animal doodles....
lion
elephant
octopus
Polar Bear
lizard
squirrel
parrot
frog

Name _____

A Place to Belong, cont.

Grassland

Desert

Rain Forest

Forest

Pond

Ocean

Arctic

Name _____

Use with page 202.

Animal Habitats

Which Body Part?

You have five senses.

Each sense has a body part that helps it work.

Which body part is used for which sense?

Write the sense on the correct line. Use the words in the box.

1. _____

2. _____

3. _____

4. _____

5. _____

see	hear	smell	taste	feel

Name _____

Use Your Senses

Do Meg's ears help her enjoy her ice cream?

When she listens to music, does she use her nose?

Read each activity on the chart.

Put an **X** in the box if the sense is used in that activity.

Add two things to the chart that you did today.

		👁	👂	👃	👄	✋
○	1. Eat ice cream					
○	2. Play a drum					
○	3. Watch a movie					
○	4. Take a bath					
○	5. Listen to music					
○	6. Hug a teddy bear					
○	7.					
○	8.					

Sniff, sniff

Name _____

A Choosy Shopper

Which foods should Meg put in her shopping cart?

She wants healthy foods to eat.

Draw pictures in the shopping cart of six of the healthiest foods.

Name _____

Healthy Eating

Take Care

Meg, Tommy, and their pets all want to be healthy.

They do important things to take care of themselves.

Use words from the **Word Box** to finish the sentences that tell good ways to take care of yourself.

1. _____ healthy food.

2. Get lots of _____ .

3. Keep your body _____ .

4. Exercise every _____ .

5. Drink plenty of _____ .

6. Keep your _____ clean.

Name _____

Good Ideas

There are some great ideas on Meg's poster for keeping healthy.
Oops! There are some unhealthy ideas, too.
Color the pictures that show healthy things.

How many unhealthy things did you find? _____

Name _____

Healthy Habits

More Good Ideas

Tom's poster is all about keeping safe.

He has shown some things that can be unsafe, too.

Put a big red **X** on the pictures that show unsafe things.

How many safe things did you find? _____

Name _____

When Seasons Change

What happens to plants in winter?

What do animals do in spring?

What is the weather like in summer?

When the seasons change, some things are different.

Draw pictures on the seasons chart.

Show some things that happen in different seasons.

Season	What is the weather?	What do animals do?	What do plants do?	What do I do?
summer				
fall				
winter				
spring				

Name _____

Hot, Cold, or In Between?

The great thing about seasons is that the temperature changes!

Meg and Tom get to do different things in different seasons.

A **thermometer** tells how hot or cold the temperature is.

Use a red crayon to color in the temperature on each thermometer.

1. The temperature is 90 °F.

2. The temperature is 60 °F.

3. The temperature is 30 °F.

4. The temperature is 70 °F.

Name _____

Three Kinds of Matter

All the things in the world are made of **matter.**

Which kind of matter is down below Meg and Aunt Betty?

A **solid** has shape and size.

A **liquid** has a size, but no shape. A liquid changes shape to fit its container. Liquids can pour.

A **gas** has no size and no shape. A gas takes the size and shape of its container.

Finish the chart to show what kind of matter each thing is made of.

	Solid	Liquid	Gas
1.			
2.			
3.			
4.			
5.			
6.			

Name _____

Forms of Matter

Solid or Liquid?

Tom really has his hands full today!

He is trying to give Tipper a bath, but it is not an easy job!

Find the solids in the picture. Color them **red.**

Find the liquids. Color them **blue.**

A **solid** has shape and size.

A **liquid** has a size,
but no shape.
A liquid changes shape.
Liquids can pour.

Name _____

Solids and Liquids

Things Are Changing

Meg is changing. She is a year older today! Look for other changes happening at Meg's party.

Write the correct word from the **Word Box** beside each number to show the cause of the change.

Word Box

bake	burn	melt
boil	freeze	mix
	expand	

1.

2.

3.

4.

5.

6.

7.

Name _____

Changes in Matter

Oh! What Air Can Do!

The balloons at Meg's party are full of air!
Air is everywhere! Air moves things!
Air fills things up! We breathe air.

The pictures show some things that air can do.
Draw two pictures of other things air can do.

1.

2.

3.

4.

5.

Name _____

How Much Air?

Air is made of different gases.
Air takes up space.
Air does not have its own shape or size.

Which has more air. . .
a full tire or a flat tire?

In each row, color the thing that has the most air.

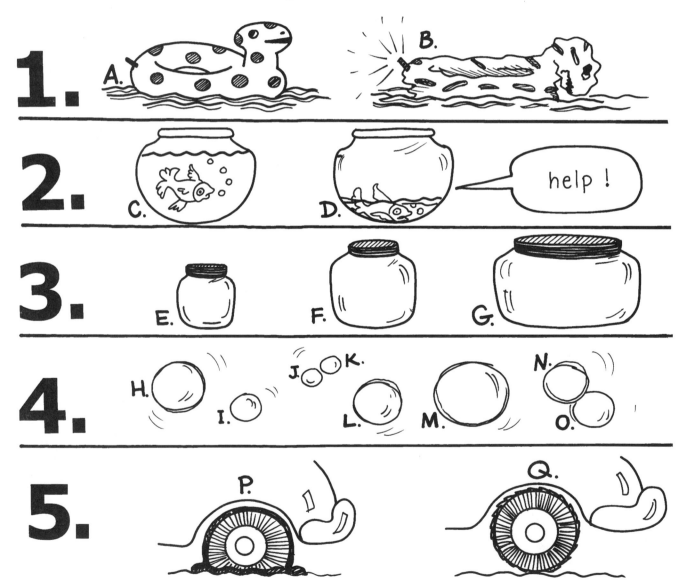

1. A. B.

2. C. D. help !

3. E. F. G.

4. H. I. J. K. L. M. N. O.

5. P. Q.

Name _____

Air Properties

Happy Floating

Rufus Rat is happy because he can float.

Fill a dishpan or sink with water.

Try to float each of these things.

Think of some other things to try to float.

Circle **yes** or **no** to show which things will float.

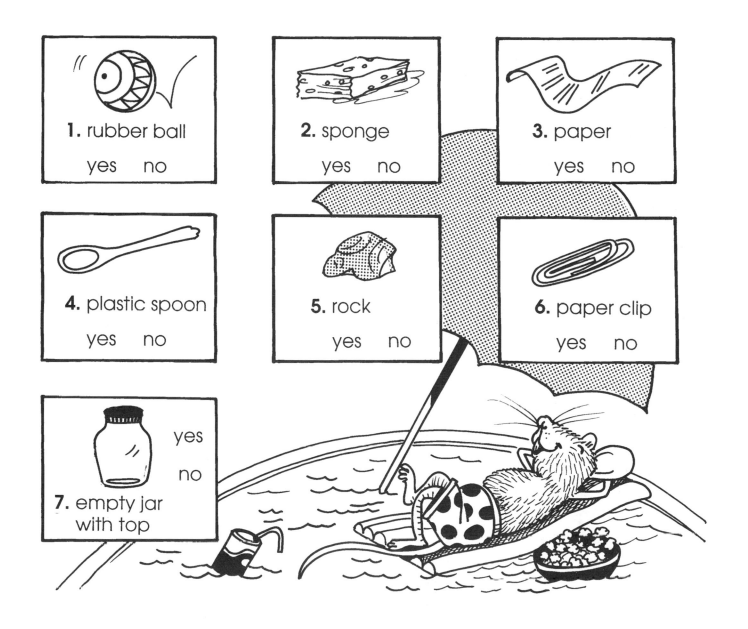

1. rubber ball

yes   no

2. sponge

yes   no

3. paper

yes   no

4. plastic spoon

yes   no

5. rock

yes   no

6. paper clip

yes   no

yes

no

7. empty jar with top

Name _____

Water Properties

X Out Pollution

All living things—including Tom and Meg—need clean, fresh air.

Unclean air causes them to be unhealthy.

Unclean air is called **polluted air.**

Make an **X** on the things that cause air pollution.

Name _____

Which Weather?

Rufus Rat needs your help.

He needs to know the name of each type of weather.

Draw a line from each picture to the right weather word.

hail	rain	wind	thunder-storm
sunshine	snow	tornado	clouds

Name _____

Pushing and Pulling

There's a lot of pulling going on in this Tug-of-War.

Pushing and pulling can move things.

A push or pull is called a **force.**

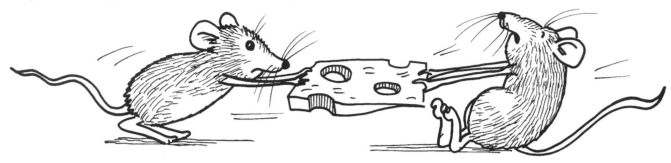

Draw an arrow to point at the force in each picture.

Circle the animal that needs more force to get moving.

Name _____

Force

A Big Attraction

Get a magnet, and collect these things.
Try to attract each one.
Does the magnet attract it? Circle **yes** or **no.**

1. plastic cup
yes   **no**

2. rubber ball
yes   **no**

3. thumbtacks
yes   **no**

4. pencil
yes   **no**

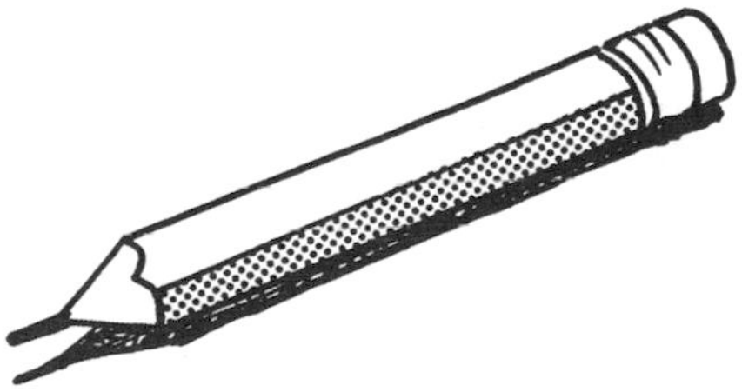

5. cracker
yes   **no**

6. paper clip
yes   **no**

7. scissors
yes   **no**

8. plastic spoon
yes   **no**

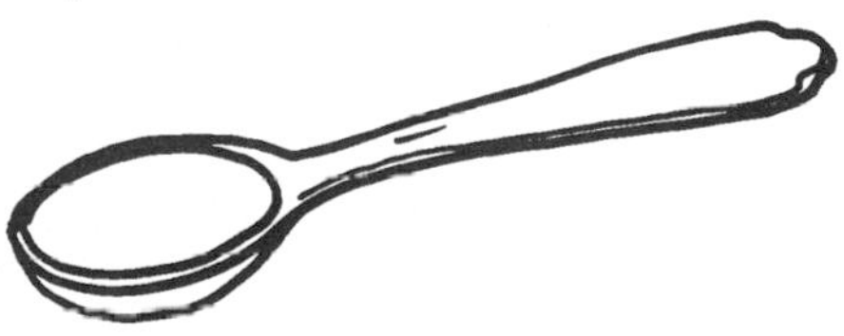

Name _____

Magnets

Scrambled Pictures

Electricity is a big word. Electricity makes many things work.

Look at the scrambled pictures.

Some things that use electricity are in this picture. Find them.

Trace the outline in red if the object uses electricity.

Trace the outline in blue if the object doesn't use electricity.

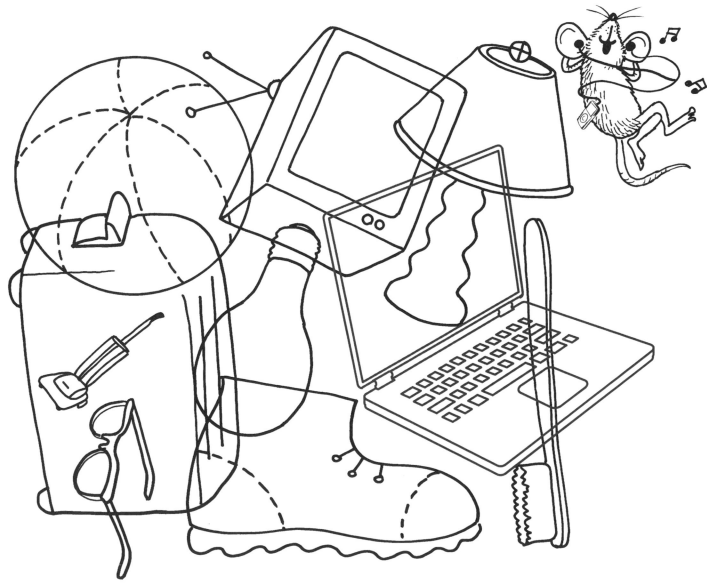

How many things that use electricity did you find? _____

Name _____

Electricity

Science Words to Know

air: Air is a mix of gases. All living things need it.

astronaut: An astronaut is a person who travels and works in space.

attract: Magnets attract some things made of metal.

body covering: The body covering is what covers a body. A bird's body covering is feathers.

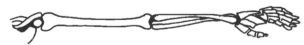

bones: Bones are hard substances that support your body. Your skeleton is made of bones.

dinosaur: Dinosaurs are reptiles that do not live on Earth anymore.

Earth: Earth is the planet where we live.

electricity: Electricity is a kind of power. A stove uses electricity to cook things.

evaporation: Evaporation happens when a liquid changes into a gas. Water evaporates into the air.

exercise: You exercise when you move your body. Exercise keeps your body strong and healthy.

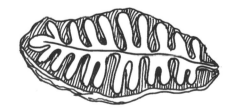

fossil: A fossil is a print or part of a plant or animal that lived long ago.

float: A boat can float on water.

flower: A flower is a plant with petals that makes seeds.

force: A push or pull is a force.

gas: A gas has no size or shape.

habitat: A habitat is the area where something lives. The bird's habitat takes care of its needs.

heart: The heart is the part of the body that pumps blood through the body.

home: A home is where an animal lives. The tree is home to these birds.

island: An island is land that has water all around it.

leaves: Leaves are a part of a plant that help it make food.

liquid: A liquid has size but no shape. A liquid can pour.

living things: Animals and plants are living things.

lungs: Lungs are a part of your body that help you breathe.

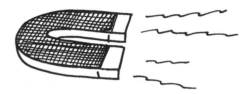

magnet: A magnet attracts some metal things.

moon: The moon is a round body that travels around the Earth.

muscles: Muscles help your body move.

ocean: An ocean is a large body of salt water. Many plants and animals live in the ocean.

planet: A planet is a body in outer space that spins around a star. Earth travels around the sun.

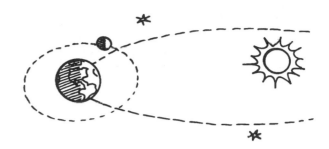

roots: The roots of a plant drink water.

seasons: Seasons are the four times of the year: summer, fall, winter, and spring.

seeds: Seeds can grow into plants.

senses: Senses help you see, feel, hear, taste, and smell.

shadow: Shadows are made when light shines on something.

solid: A solid has a shape and size.

space: Earth, the moon, the sun, and the stars are out in space.

star: A star is made of gas and gives off light. The sun is a star.

stem: The stem holds up a plant.

valley: A valley is a low place between mountains or hills.

water: Water is a liquid.

waves: The ocean has waves.

weather: The weather can be sunny or cloudy.

wind: Wind is moving air.

MATH

Skills Exercises
Grade One

SKILLS CHECKLIST
NUMBERS & COUNTING

✔	SKILL	PAGE(S)
	Count to numbers less than 100	230–232, 234, 235, 249
	Count to 100	233, 236
	Skip count by 2	234
	Skip count by 5	235
	Skip count by 10	236
	Read and use ordinals	237
	Match numbers to sets and models	238, 239
	Read and write numbers on number lines	240, 241
	Match numerals to word names	242, 243
	Writing and ordering numbers	244
	Read and write whole numbers to 5 digits	244
	Read and write numbers in expanded form	245
	Identify place value through hundreds	245–247
	Compare amounts using comparison words	248, 249
	Compare whole numbers using < and >	249
	Order whole numbers	250
	Round numbers to the nearest ten	251
	Explore big numbers	252
	Estimate numbers of objects	253
	Identify values of coins	254, 255
	Count money	255
	Match fractions to pictures and models	256–258
	Read, write, and illustrate simple fractions	256–258
	Compare fractions	258
	Tell time to the half hour	259–261
	Find numbers and information on a calendar	262
	Measure length	263
	Recognize units for measuring length, weight, and capacity	263–265

SKILLS CHECKLIST
MATH COMPUTATION & PROBLEM SOLVING

✔	SKILL	PAGE(S)
	Add sets of objects	268, 270
	Answer questions from diagrams and pictures	268–270, 289, 305–310
	Add whole numbers	268, 270–272, 274, 275, 277–285, 287–289, 291–294
	Subtract sets of objects	269
	Use addition and subtraction facts through 20	271–286, 288
	Subtract whole numbers	269, 271, 273, 276, 277–283, 300, 301, 304
	Find missing numbers in number sentences	277, 279–282, 309
	Add and subtract with zero	283
	Add 3 numbers	284–285
	Choose correct operation for a problem	286
	Add 2-digit numbers	287–289, 291–292
	Recognize fact families; find missing facts	287
	Write number sentences to match models	289, 290, 305
	Subtract 2-digit numbers	290–291
	Add and subtract 10	292–294
	Add and subtract multiples of 10	293–294
	Identify amounts of money	295–298
	Solve problems with money	295–298
	Use a variety of problem-solving strategies	295–313
	Identify value of coins	296–298
	Do a variety of time-telling tasks	299–303
	Solve problems with time	299–303
	Answer questions from data on graphs and charts	304–306
	Solve simple word problems	308–310
	Explain how a problem was solved	312, 313

More & More Marbles

Do you think little dinosaurs play marbles in their caves?

Explore the cave.

Find all the marbles, and color them different colors.

Count the marbles. How many did you find? _____

Name _____

Counting

Fun Run

Take a run with these joggers.

Watch out for the little animals on the path!

Color all the animals, and then count them.

1. How many ? ☐

2. How many ? ☐

3. How many ? ☐

4. How many ? ☐

5. How many ? ☐

6. How many  ? ☐

Name _____

Splash Down

It's Turtle Fun Day at Water Slide Park.

Color the ladder different colors.

Walk your fingers up the ladder to count the steps.

How many are there? [ ] Then slide down with the turtles.

wheeee

Wow

Whoops

Water

Go up again. How many steps did you count this time? [ ]

Color the turtles.

Name _____

Counting

Trampoline Trouble

Fran and Felix want to jump **100** times on the trampoline.

Write in the missing numbers so they can jump on each number.

Use your fingers to jump to each number.

Say the numbers as you jump.

If you make a mistake, climb on and try again.

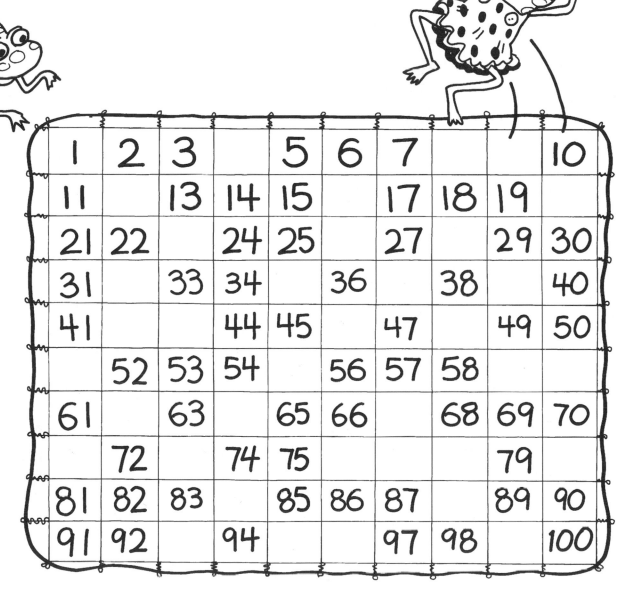

1	2	3		5	6	7			10
11		13	14	15		17	18	19	
21	22		24	25		27		29	30
31		33	34		36		38		40
41			44	45		47		49	50
	52	53	54		56	57	58		
61		63		65	66		68	69	70
	72		74	75				79	
81	82	83		85	86	87		89	90
91	92		94			97	98		100

Color Fran and Felix.

Name _____

Double Doubles

The Bunny Hop twins do everything by twos.

What are they doing today?

Count by twos, and draw a line from one number to the next.

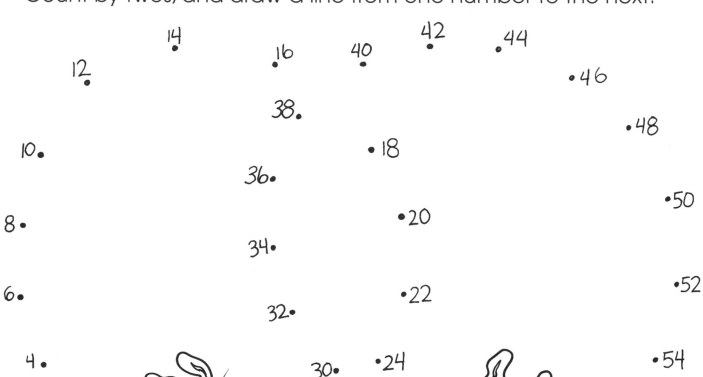

Color the twins. How high did you count? [ ]

Name _____

High Fives

What a game! Each player bounces the ball 5 times.

Count by fives.

Write the missing numbers on the players' shirts.

What is the highest number you counted? ☐

Which 2 players are making a "high five"? ☐ and ☐

Color the picture.

Name _____

Skip Counting by 5

100-Yard Dash

Kerry Kangaroo always hops by tens.

Help her hop 10 times to get to 100.

Count by tens and write in the missing numbers.

Color Kerry's path.

Name _____

Skip Counting by 10

The Winner Is . . .

The race is almost over.

The first 5 runners are crossing the finish line.

Draw a line from each runner to the ribbon he will get.

Color the winning turtle green.

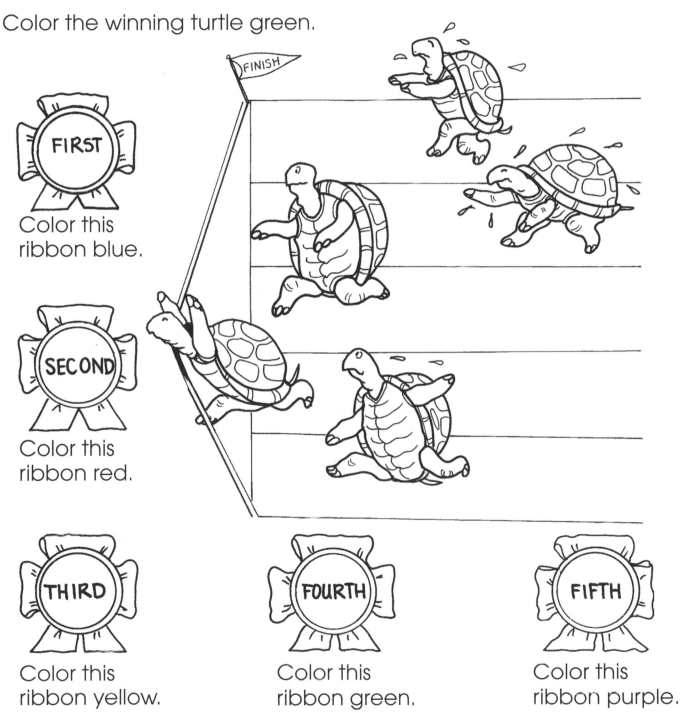

FIRST

Color this ribbon blue.

SECOND

Color this ribbon red.

THIRD

Color this ribbon yellow.

FOURTH

Color this ribbon green.

FIFTH

Color this ribbon purple.

Name _____

Under the Sea

Help Diver Dan count the fish in 4 schools!

A school of fish is a group of the same kind of fish that swim together.

Color the school of **11** fish **yellow.**   Color the school of **21** fish **red.**

Color the school of **19** fish **purple.**   Color the school of **7** fish **orange.**

Name _____

Matching Numbers to Sets

A Messy Room

Abby's sports things are all over her room.

Some things are missing.

Read the total number for each group.

Draw the missing things.

4 footballs

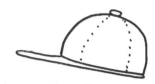

2 baseball caps

11 hockey pucks

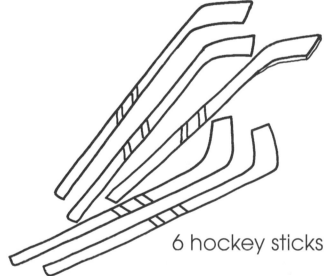

6 hockey sticks

3 baseball bats

7 golf balls

Color Abby.

Name _____

Matching Numbers to Sets

Long Jumpers

Three very good jumpers are having a contest.

Who can jump the farthest?

Look at the number line to see how far each one has jumped.

1. jumped ☐ feet.

2. jumped ☐ feet.

3. jumped ☐ feet.

Draw yourself on the number line jumping 25 feet.

Did you jump farther than the 🐰 ? **yes** **no**

Did 🐰 jump farther than the 🦘 ? **yes** **no**

Did 🐸 jump farther than the 🐰 ? **yes** **no**

Color all the jumpers.

Name _____

Using a Number Line

Ladybug Marathon

The ladybugs make a nice number line.

Use your fingers to walk the number line.

Answer each ladybug's question when you land on her.

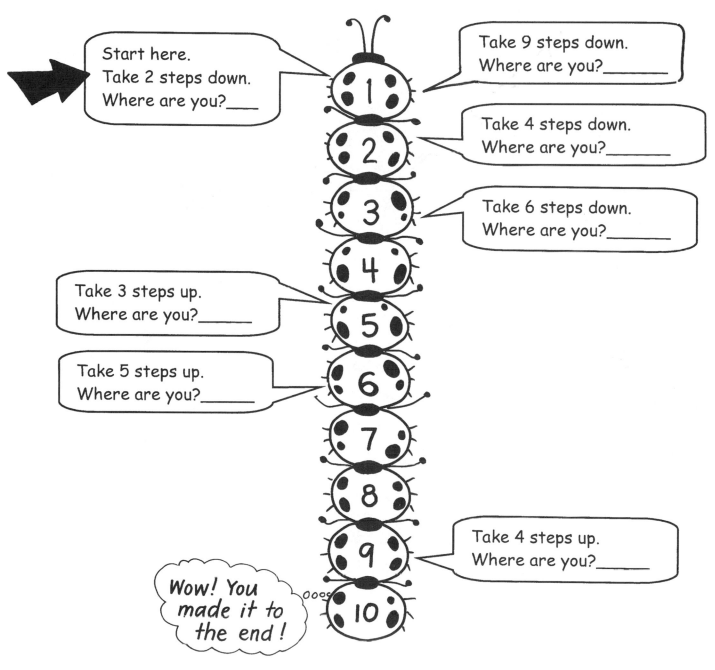

Start here.
Take 2 steps down.
Where are you?____

Take 9 steps down.
Where are you?_____

Take 4 steps down.
Where are you?_____

Take 6 steps down.
Where are you?_____

Take 3 steps up.
Where are you?_____

Take 5 steps up.
Where are you?_____

Take 4 steps up.
Where are you?_____

Wow! You made it to the end!

Color the ladybugs.

Name _____

Swim for It

At the Animal Olympics, 6 swimmers are lined up for the big race.
Help them get ready to swim!
Follow the directions.

1. Draw goggles ⌐○○⌐ on the swimmer in lane three.

2. Color the swimmer in lane five yellow.

3. Draw teeth on the swimmer in lane one.

4. Make the swimmer in lane six come out of his shell.

5. Draw a hat on the swimmer in lane two.

6. Color the swimmer in lane four brown.

Name _____

Matching Numerals to Words

Too Many Players

A soccer team has eleven players.

Does this team have the right number? _No_

Read the numbers on the shirts.

Write the numbers beside the matching words.

1. [15] fifteen
2. [12] twelve
3. [71] seventy-one
4. [33] thirty-three

5. [13] thirteen
6. [51] fifty-one
7. [90] ninety
8. [62] sixty-two

9. [17] seventeen
10. [8] eight
11. [50] fifty
12. [26] twenty-six

Name _____

Matching Numerals to Words

Fishing for Sixes

Cousin Cary Cat is fishing for catfish.

He has 6 fat catfish on his line.

How many pounds does each fish weigh?

Write the correct number on each fish.

296   16   **66**

6,000   660   6

Color the heaviest fish orange.

Color the other fish any colors.

Name _____

Writing Numbers

A Long, Hot Run

These runners are very thirsty.

They have run a long way on a hot day.

They need to drink a lot of water.

Bonnie ran for 147 minutes. $147 = 100 + 40 + 7$

Barney ran for 199 minutes. $199 = 100 + 90 + 9$

Ben ran for 84 minutes. $84 = 80 + 4$

Look at the times for the other runners. Draw a line to the glass of water that shows what the number means.

1. 89 minutes   2. 96 minutes   3. 133 minutes

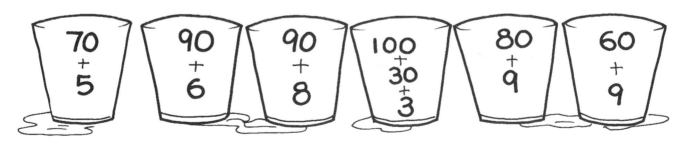

4. 75 minutes   5. 69 minutes   6. 98 minutes

Color the runners.

Name _____

Writing Numbers • Expanded Notation

A Pogo Puzzle

Polly and Pagoo are on a pogo stick team.

They bounce many times.

The words tell how many times they bounce.

Write the numbers to match the words.

Then color Polly and Pagoo.

Across
A. 2 tens, 3 ones
C. 1 hundred, 0 tens, 0 ones
D. 8 tens, 7 ones
E. 6 tens, 5 ones
F. 9 tens, 2 ones
G. 4 tens, 1 one
H. 6 tens, 0 ones

Down
A. 2 tens, 0 ones
B. 3 tens, 0 ones
C. 1 ten, 7 ones
D. 8 tens, 5 ones
E. 6 tens, 6 ones
F. 9 tens, 1 one
G. 4 tens, 0 ones

Name _____

Writing Numbers • Place Value

A Hidden Sport

Sara is happy about a game she has won.

But what is her sport?

A clue is hiding in the puzzle.

Follow the code to color the spaces.

Find out what is hiding.

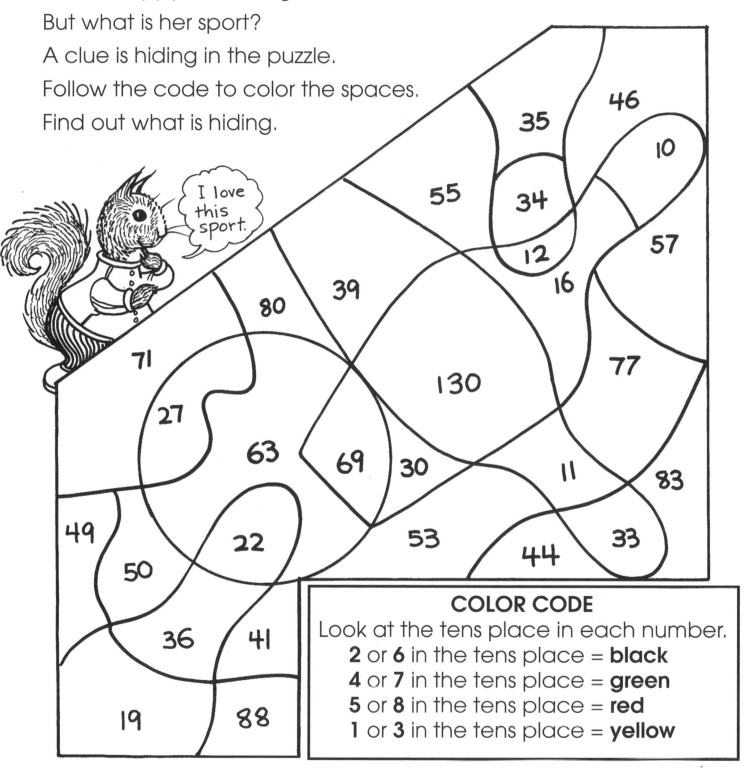

I love this sport.

COLOR CODE

Look at the tens place in each number.

2 or **6** in the tens place = **black**

4 or **7** in the tens place = **green**

5 or **8** in the tens place = **red**

1 or **3** in the tens place = **yellow**

Name _____

Place Value

Hula Hoop Dancers

The hula hoop dancers are dancing on the sand.
They dance and spin 1 or more hoops.
But where are their hoops?

Follow the directions to draw the hoops.

1. Draw a red hula hoop on the shortest dancer.

2. Draw a blue hula hoop on the dancer with the longest skirt.

3. Draw an orange hula hoop on the dancer with the most coconuts.

4. Draw a green hula hoop on the dancer with the fewest necklaces.

5. Draw a purple hula hoop on the dancer with the most necklaces.

6. Draw a yellow hula hoop on the dancer with the fewest coconuts.

Name _____

Comparing Numbers

Headed for Trouble

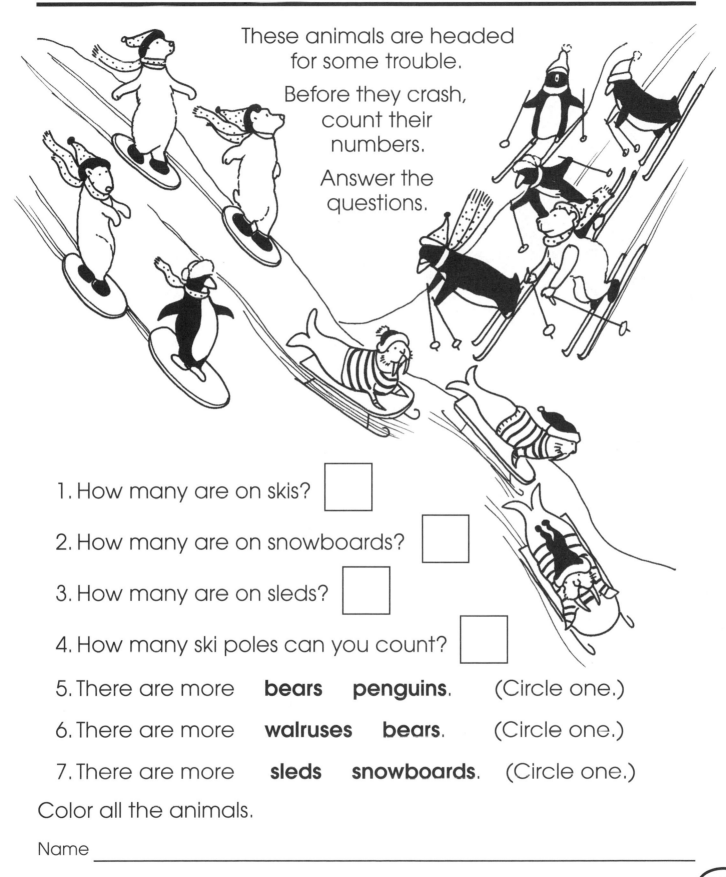

These animals are headed for some trouble.

Before they crash, count their numbers.

Answer the questions.

1. How many are on skis?   ☐

2. How many are on snowboards?   ☐

3. How many are on sleds?   ☐

4. How many ski poles can you count?   ☐

5. There are more   **bears**   **penguins**.   (Circle one.)

6. There are more   **walruses**   **bears**.   (Circle one.)

7. There are more   **sleds**   **snowboards**.   (Circle one.)

Color all the animals.

Name _____

Comparing Numbers • Counting

Monkey Business

This monkey is a long way from his home in the jungle.

Connect the dots to find out where he is and what he is doing.

Connect the dots by putting the numbers in order from 1 to 38.

Color the picture.

Name _____

Ordering Numbers

Round-Up Rodeo

Get out your lasso!

Join the Round-Up Rodeo!

Help Cowboy Carl round the numbers.

Color all the multiples of 10 blue.

Pick 10 numbers that are not colored.

Write each number on a line below.

Round each number to the nearest 10.

Round **UP** numbers that end in **5** or more.
Round **DOWN** numbers that end in **4** or less.

Number	Number Rounded		Number	Number Rounded
1. _____	_____		6. _____	_____
2. _____	_____		7. _____	_____
3. _____	_____		8. _____	_____
4. _____	_____		9. _____	_____
5. _____	_____		10. _____	_____

Color the cowboy and his horse.

1	2	3	4	5
6	7	8	9	10
11	12	13	14	15
16	17	18	19	20
21	22	23	24	25
26	27	28	29	30
31	32	33	34	35
36	37	38	39	40
41	42	43	44	45
46	47	48	49	50
51	52	53	54	55
56	57	58	59	60
61	62	63	64	65
66	67	68	69	70
71	72	73	74	75
76	77	78	79	80
81	82	83	84	85
86	87	88	89	90
91	92	93	94	95
96	97	98	99	
		100		

Name _____

Rounding

Table Tennis Terror

There has been an accident at the table tennis ball factory.

The table tennis balls are bursting out the door!

Quick! Draw a line from each ball to the matching number as the balls go past you.

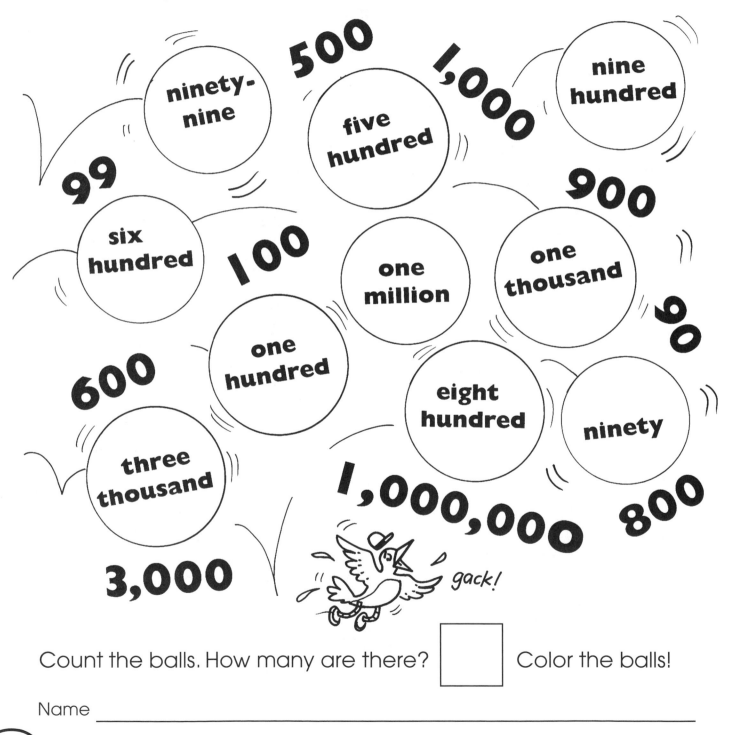

Count the balls. How many are there? ☐ Color the balls!

Name _____

Hide-and-Seek

The Mousekin kids are playing hide-and-seek in their room.
Take a quick look at the picture. Then close your eyes.
Estimate how many hiding places the mice have found.

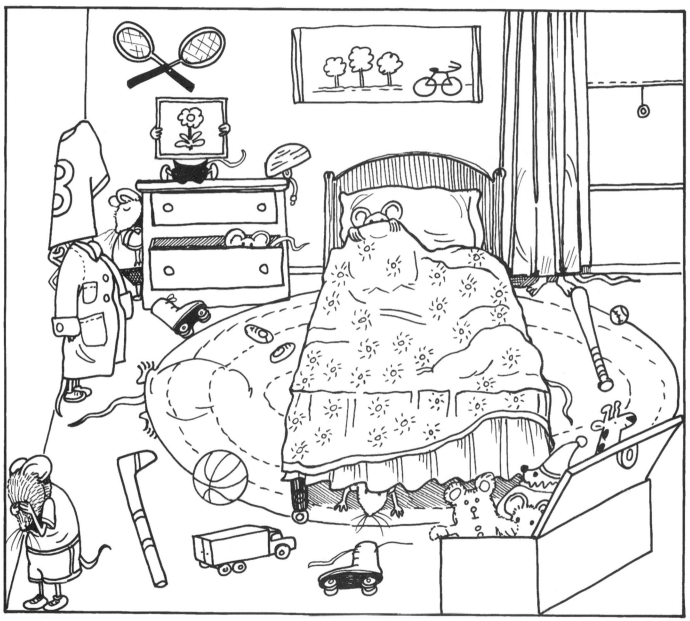

How many did you estimate? ☐   Now count the hidden mice.

How many did you find? ☐   Color the picture.

Name _____

Find a Penny

Lucky Penny likes to search the beach for lost coins.
She puts the coins in her piggy banks.

"Find a penny
Pick it up
All the day
You'll have good luck!"

Write the names of the coins on the lines.

Write the amount for each coin on the piggy bank.

penny _____ ¢ one cent

nickel _____ ¢ five cents

dime _____ ¢ ten cents

quarter _____ ¢ twenty-five cents

Color Lucky Penny.

Name _____

Value of Coins

Find a Penny, cont.

Count the money.

1. On Monday, Lucky Penny found

_____ ¢

2. On Wednesday, she found

_____ ¢

3. On Friday, she found

_____ ¢

4. On Saturday, she found

$ _____ . _____

How much money did Lucky find this week? $ _____ . _____

Color Lucky Penny.

Name _____

Counting Money

A Very Hungry Hockey Player

Hannah is very hungry after the hockey game.
She goes to the pizza shop and eats lots of pizza.
Help the pizza shop put toppings on the pizza.

pepperoni   pineapple   olives

1. Draw pepperoni
   on one half.

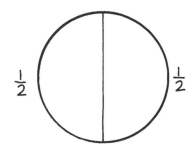

2. Draw pineapple
   on one quarter.

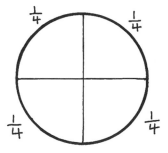

3. Draw olives
   on one eighth.

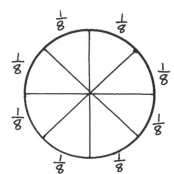

4. Draw your favorite
   toppings on one sixth.

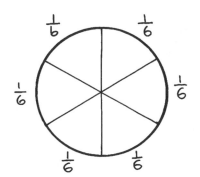

Name _____

Fractions

The 3-Legged Race

Help the mice find their trails for the 3-legged race.

Millie and Mary follow a trail of halves.

Use a blue crayon to connect all the ways to show $\frac{1}{2}$.

Mike and Mac follow a trail of fourths.

Use a red crayon to connect all the ways to show $\frac{1}{4}$.

THREE-LEGGED RACE

one half

one quarter

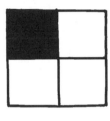

$\frac{1}{2}$

$\frac{1}{4}$

one fourth

Finish Time: $\frac{1}{2}$ hour, or 30 minutes

Finish Time: $\frac{1}{4}$ hour, or 15 minutes

Color the mice.

Name _____

Fractions

First Prize for Yummy Pies

Today is the pie-eating contest.

The pies are yummy, and the pie eaters are very full.

Look at the sizes of the pie pieces that are left.

1. Draw a box around the fraction that shows the biggest piece.

2. Draw a circle around the fraction that shows the smallest piece.

3. What is your favorite kind of pie? _____

4. Which size piece would you like to eat? _____

Color the picture.

Name _____

Comparing Fractions

They're Off!

The horses are ready!

The clock shows what time the race will start.

Write the missing numbers on the clock.

Then complete the sentences.

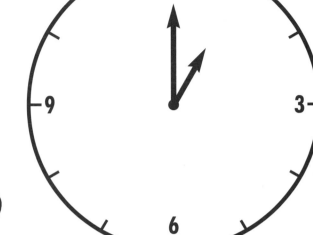

On your mark, get set...

HEY! He didn't say "GO" yet!

I'm off!

1. The minute hand is on the ☐ .

2. The hour hand is on the ☐ .

3. The time is ☐ : ☐ .

4. In $\frac{1}{2}$ hour it will be ☐ : ☐ .

Color the picture.

Name _____

Telling Time

Snow Time

Snow days are fun from morning until night.

Kids can think of fun things to do all day long.

Write the time that is shown on each clock.

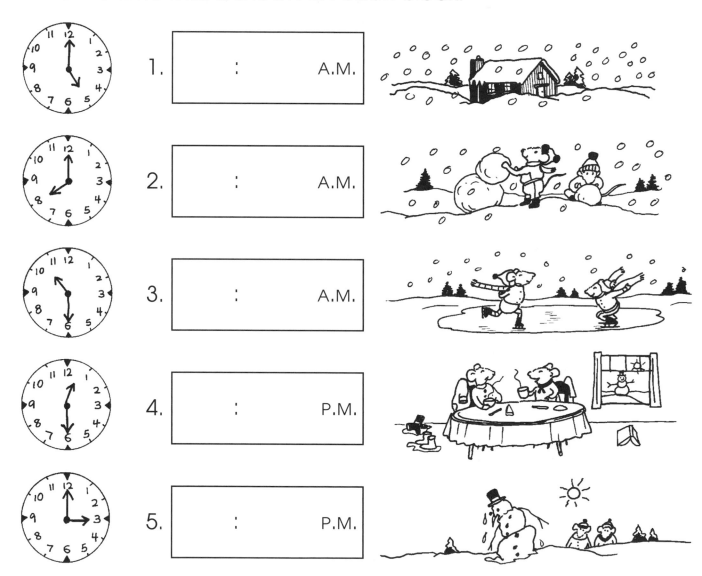

1. _____ : _____ A.M.

2. _____ : _____ A.M.

3. _____ : _____ A.M.

4. _____ : _____ P.M.

5. _____ : _____ P.M.

6. _____ : _____ P.M.

Color the pictures.

Name _____

Show Time

The shows are starting! Don't be late!
Read about each show and follow the directions.

1. The marching band starts a show at 3:00. It lasts 30 minutes.
   Draw the hands on the clock to show the time it will end.

  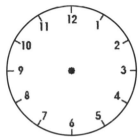

2. The rodeo starts at 4:00. It lasts for 1 hour.
   Draw the hands on the clock to show the time it will end.

  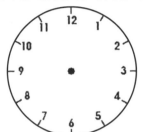 

3. The ice show starts at 5:30. It lasts for 1 hour.
   Draw the hands on the clock to show the time it will end.

   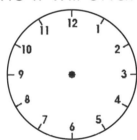

4. The water show starts at 7:00. It lasts for 30 minutes.
   Draw the hands on the clock to show the time it will end.

  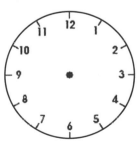

Color the pictures.

Name _____

Telling Time

Fantastic Gymnastics

Ari loves gymnastics.
He goes to the gym every Tuesday to practice.
He practices some other days, too.

Look at Ari's calendar.
Fill in the missing numbers.

FEBRUARY						
Sun.	Mon.	Tues	Wed.	Thurs.	Fri.	Sat.
1	2	3 gym		5	gym	7
8	9	10 gym	11		13	
15		gym	18	gym	20	gym
22		24 gym		meet	27	

1. Write the dates of all the Tuesdays. _____, _____, _____, _____

2. How many Tuesdays are there? _____

3. How many days are there from one Tuesday to the next?
   (Count each day of the week only once.) _____

4. Is the gymnastics meet on a Wednesday? **yes no** (Circle one.)

5. Valentine's Day is February 14th. Draw a heart on that day.

   Color Ari.

   Name _____

Walking Tall

These friends can walk tall on their stilts.

Let's hope they don't fall off!

The tall stilts are fun to measure.

Use an inch ruler to measure all the things below.

(Round to the nearest half inch.)

1. ears

in.

2. stilts

in.

6. beak

in.

3. tail

in.

4. legs

in.

9. neck

in.

7. antennae

in.

5. stilts

in.

8. stilts

in.

10. legs

in.

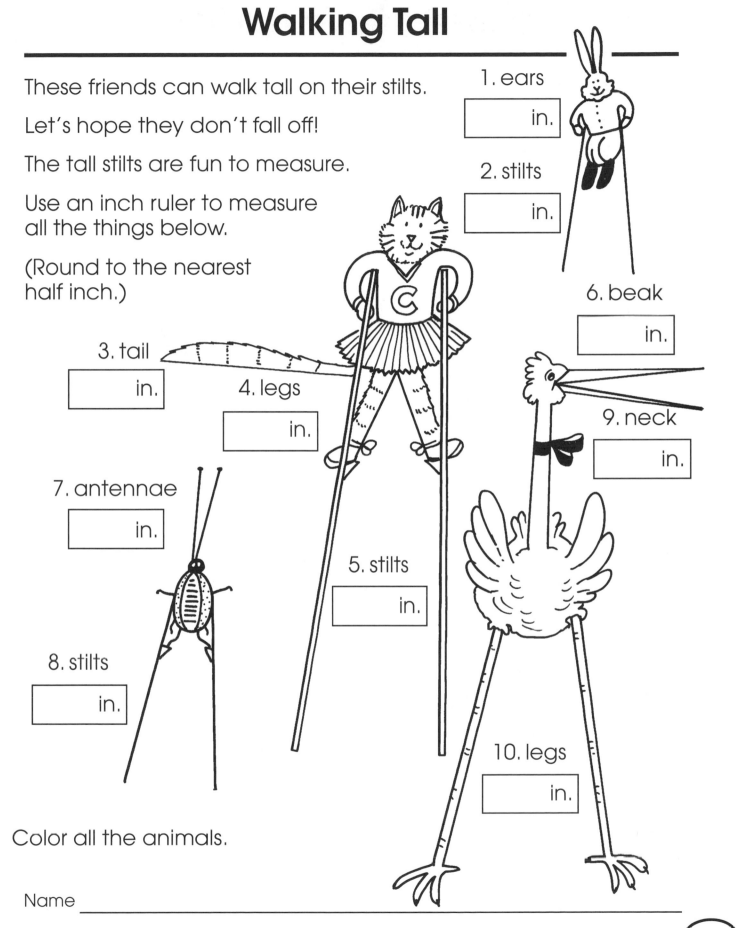

Color all the animals.

Name _____

Measuring Length

Some Heavy Lifting

Willy the Weight Lifter is a little lopsided.
One barbell has **ounces,** and the other has **pounds.**
Ounces and pounds are very different weights.
It takes 16 ounces to make 1 pound.

An apple weighs a few ounces.
A pair of shoes weighs about a pound.

Circle ounces or pounds to
measure each of these things.

1. **Will's cookies**

   ounces   pounds

2. **Will's telephone book**

   ounces   pounds

3. **Will's jug of milk**

   ounces   pounds

4. **Will's pencil**

   ounces   pounds

5. **Will's hat**

   ounces   pounds

6. **Will's big barbell**

   ounces   pounds

7. **Will's friend, Oscar**

   ounces   pounds

8. **Will's grapes**

   ounces   pounds

Color the pictures.

Name _____

Units for Measuring Weight

A Great Sand Castle

Sandy Squirrel has built a sand castle for a contest at the beach.
She deserves a blue ribbon for the most beautiful sand castle.
What did she use to make the castle?
She used a cup and a pail.

The pail holds 1 gallon.
The cup holds 1 cup.

A gallon = 16 cups.

1 cup

Color the sand castle.

Then use a crayon
to circle the true sentences.

1. The pail holds less than the cup.

2. The cup holds more than 1 gallon.

3. 1 gallon is more than 1 cup.

4. The cup holds less than 1 gallon.

5. The pail holds less than 1 cup.

6. 4 cups make a gallon.

7. 4 gallons equal 1 cup.

8. The big part of the sand castle was made with a cup.

Name _____

Units for Measuring Capacity

Math Words to Know

clock: A clock tells time. This clock shows a time of 7:30.

coins: Coins are worth an amount of money.

penny = 1¢   nickel = 5¢

dime = 10¢   quarter = 25¢

digit: Numbers have 1 or more digits. This number has 3 digits.

529

fraction: A fraction shows a part of something. This picture shows that $\frac{1}{3}$ of the pie is gone.

half: Two halves make a whole thing. This pizza is half gone. Half is a fraction: $\frac{1}{2}$

hundreds: The third place from the right in a number is the hundreds place. In this number, the 8 is in the hundreds place.

853

length: Length measures something along a line. The length of this worm is 3 inches.

measure: People measure to find out how long, big, or heavy something is or to find how much something holds. The lion uses a scale to measure his weight.

number line: A number line shows numbers in order along a line.

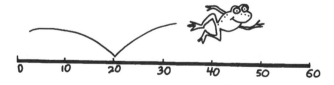

ones: The first place from the right in a number is the ones place. In this number there are 6 ones.

276

place value: Place value tells the size of each digit in a number.

524

5 is in the hundreds place.
2 is in the tens place.
4 is in the ones place.

pound: The weight of things can be measured in pounds. A heavy pair of shoes weighs about 5 pounds.

quarter: There are 4 quarters in a whole thing. A quarter is a fraction, written $\frac{1}{4}$. One quarter of this pie is missing.

set: A set is a group of things you can count. This set has 6 things.

skip counting: To skip count, you skip over some numbers. Counting 2, 4, 6, 8, 10, 12 is skip counting by twos.

2 4 6 8 10 12

tens: The tens place from the right is the second place in a number. In this number, 7 is in the tens place.

672

third: There are three thirds in a whole thing. One third is a fraction, written $\frac{1}{3}$. This shape is $\frac{1}{3}$ spotted.

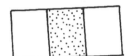

time: Clocks measure time. There are 60 seconds in a minute. There are 60 minutes in an hour. There are 24 hours in a day.

weight: Weight tells how heavy something is. Weight can be measured in ounces or pounds. This weight lifter is lifting 150 pounds.

She Sells Seashells

What a surprise! An octopus is selling seashells on the seashore!

Leo comes out of the water to look at Sandy's shells.

Count the shells in each box.

Then help Leo solve the problems.

Write the missing numbers.

1. 🐚 + ⭐ = ☐

2. 🦪 + 🐚 = ☐

3. 🐚 + 🐚 = ☐

4. ✳ + 🦪 = ☐

Name _____

Add Sets

Jingo's Short Jog

Oh, oh! Jingo forgot about his jogging!

He stopped to look at the animals along the way.

As he watched, some of them crawled or flew away.

How many are left?

Jingo saw two lizards. One crawled away.

$$\text{(two lizards)} - \text{(one lizard)} = \boxed{1}$$

Write the answers.

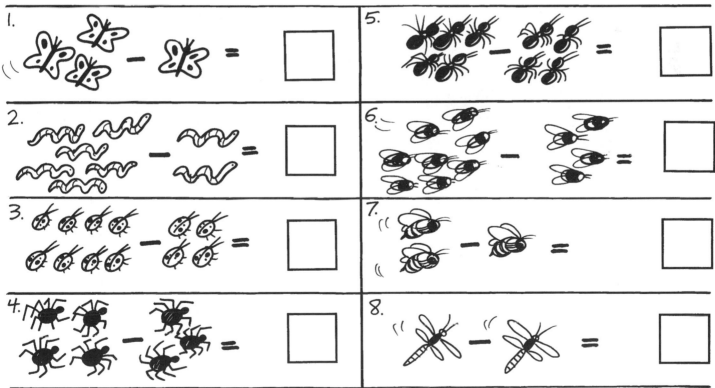

1.

2.

3.

4.

5.

6.

7.

8.

Name _____

Subtract Sets

Lost Golf Balls

Dizzy and Daisy Dinosaur are looking for golf balls in the swamp.
Help them count the golf balls.
Then answer the questions.

1. How many golf balls are in the water? ☐

2. How many balls are in their hands? ☐

3. How many are on the land? ☐

4. Can you write a number sentence to tell the story?

   ☐ on the land + ☐ in the water + ☐ in hand = ☐ golf balls

Color the animals and the golf balls.

Name _____

Add with Sets

Lost Marbles

Suzie's favorite game is marbles.

She has invited 7 friends to join her for a game.

She started the first game with 12 marbles.

She lost 3 marbles.

Now she has 9 marbles, because 12 – 3 = 9.

Use math facts you know to fill in the missing numbers in the chart.

	Marbles To Start	Marbles Lost	Marbles Left
Suzie had	12	3	9
Elvis had	9	8	
Dino had	11	4	
Dinah had	8	5	
Danny had		7	5
Sally had		6	6
Emma had	11		6
Rico had		3	7

Write the answers.

1. Danny started with ☐ marbles.

2. Emma lost ☐ marbles.

3. Dino finished with ☐ marbles.

4. Sally started with ☐ marbles.

5. Rico started with ☐ marbles.

6. ☐ lost the most marbles.

Name _____

Lost in the Web

Spiro Spider has lots of shoes caught in his web. Help him find his lost hiking boot. Write all the answers to the problems. Then use the **Color Code** to color the shoes and boots. The red boot is the one Spiro has lost.

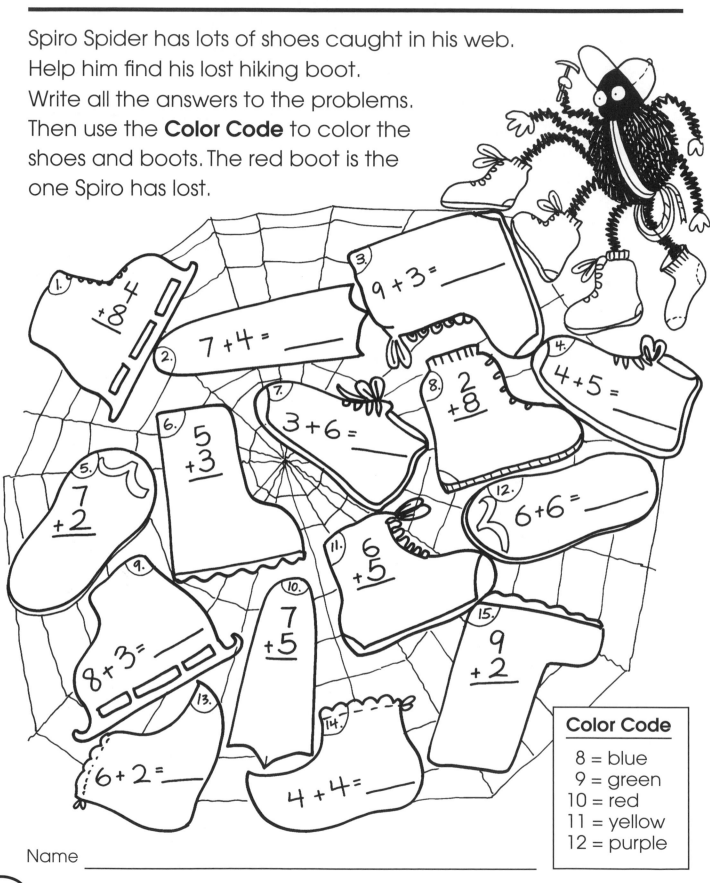

1. 4
   $+8$

2. $7 + 4 =$ ___

3. $9 + 3 =$ ___

4. $4 + 5 =$ ___

5. 7
   $+2$

6. 5
   $+3$

7. $3 + 6 =$ ___

8. 2
   $+8$

9. $8 + 3 =$ ___

10. 7
    $+5$

11. 6
    $+5$

12. $6 + 6 =$ ___

13. $6 + 2 =$ ___

14. $4 + 4 =$ ___

15. 9
    $+2$

Color Code

8 = blue
9 = green
10 = red
11 = yellow
12 = purple

Name ___

Addition Facts through 12

The Mud Pie Fight

It is such fun for Lulu and Larry to throw mud pies!
Finish the facts on the mud pies to find out who threw the most.
Lulu's pies have answers that are even numbers.
Larry's have answers that are odd numbers.
Count the pies and write the scores in the score box.

It's an icky, sticky, mud fest!

Lulu
EVEN

1. 10 – 2 = _____
2. 16 – 6 = _____
3. 15 – 4 = _____
4. 18 – 7 = _____
5. 17 – 6 = _____
6. 12 – 6 = _____
7. 18 – 9 = _____
8. 13 – 7 = _____
9. 16 – 7 = _____
10. 16 – 8 = _____
11. 11 – 3 = _____
12. 17 – 10 = _____
13. 12 – 3 = _____
14. 11 – 5 = _____
15. 14 – 9 = _____
16. 15 – 6 = _____

It's a yucky, mucky mud fling!

Larry
ODD

Who threw the most pies?

_____

- -

_____

Name _____

Lulu	
Larry	

Subtraction Facts through 18

Fishy Facts

Felix has been fishing for facts. He has a great catch!
Write the answers for all the fishy facts.
Then use the **Color Code** to color Felix's fish.

Color Code

14 = red
15 = green
16 = blue
17 = orange
18 = purple

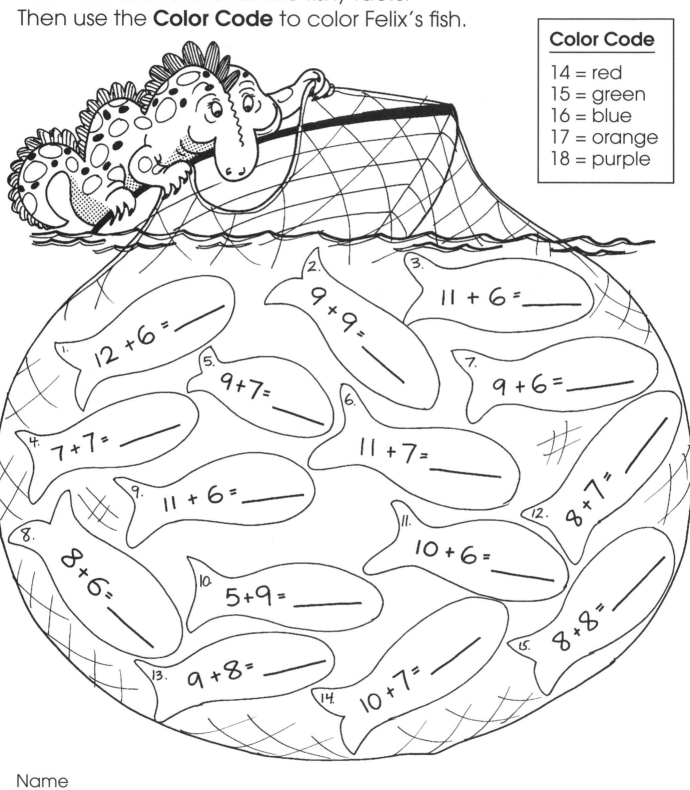

1. 12 + 6 = ___
2. 9 + 9 = ___
3. 11 + 6 = ___
4. 7 + 7 = ___
5. 9 + 7 = ___
6. 11 + 7 = ___
7. 9 + 6 = ___
8. 8 + 6 = ___
9. 11 + 6 = ___
10. 5 + 9 = ___
11. 10 + 6 = ___
12. 8 + 7 = ___
13. 9 + 8 = ___
14. 10 + 7 = ___
15. 8 + 8 = ___

Name _____

Addition Facts through 18

Skateboard Fun

The creatures are having such fun on their skateboards!

Dixon the dinosaur is letting them use his back for their ride.

Use the clues to solve the puzzle.

Write the answer to each number fact in the correct spaces.

CLUES

Across			Down	
A. 10 + 9	D. 10 + 10	G. 7 + 7	A. 9 + 7	F. 6 + 8
B. 8 + 8	E. 7 + 6	H. 5 + 7	C. 4 + 6	G. 5 + 6
C. 9 + 9	F. 8 + 9		E. 8 + 7	H. 2 + 8

Name _____

Addition Facts through 20

Thirsty Runners

9 runners ran 9 miles.
They dried off with 9 towels.

They drank 9 bottles of juice
and ate 9 candy bars.

All these problems
are about 9.

Find the answers.

1. 12
   $-\ 9$
   3 ✓

2. 18
   $-\ 9$
   9

3. 10
   $+\ 9$
   19 ✓

4. 13
   $-\ 9$
   04 ✓

5. 16
   $-\ 9$
   7 ✓

6. 9
   $+\ 4$
   13 ✓

7. 9
   $+\ 5$
   14

8. 15
   $-\ 9$
   6 ✓

9. 10
   $-\ 9$
   1 ✓

10. 17
   -9
   08 ✓

11. 16
   $-\ 9$
   07 ✓

12. 12
   $-\ 3$
   09

13. 9
   $-\ 1$
   8 ✓

14. 11
   $-\ 9$
   02 ✓

15. 14
   $-\ 9$
   05 ✓

16. 9
   $+\ 9$
   18 ✓

17. 9
   $-\ 0$
   9 ✓

18. 9
   $-\ 9$
   0 ✓

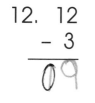
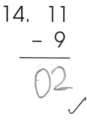
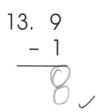
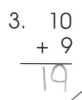
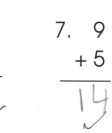

Name _____

Addition & Subtraction Facts with 9

Help!

6 families are worried! A family member has fallen out of each raft. All the rafts are full of fact families. Look at the problems on the side of each raft.

Decide what number is missing from both problems. Draw a line from each raft to its lost family member.

1. $6 + \square = 10$
   $10 - \square = 6$

2. $12 - 3 = \square$
   $\square + 3 = 12$

3. $2 + \square = 7$
   $7 - 2 = \square$

4. $11 - \square = 5$
   $5 + \square = 11$

5. $13 - \square = 6$
   $\square + 6 = 13$

6. $17 - \square = 9$
   $9 + \square = 17$

Name _____

Floating Away

Bert was selling balloons at the ballpark.
That was before a big wind came along and blew him away!
Write the answers on his balloons to
help him sink back to Earth. Then
follow the **Color Code**
to color the
balloons.

3.
$$\begin{array}{r} 16 \\ -9 \\ \hline \end{array}$$

4.
$$\begin{array}{r} 6 \\ +7 \\ \hline \end{array}$$

1.
$$\begin{array}{r} 7 \\ +9 \\ \hline \end{array}$$

2.
$$\begin{array}{r} 8 \\ +9 \\ \hline \end{array}$$

7.
$$\begin{array}{r} 11 \\ -4 \\ \hline \end{array}$$

8.
$$\begin{array}{r} 8 \\ +8 \\ \hline \end{array}$$

5.
$$\begin{array}{r} 12 \\ -5 \\ \hline \end{array}$$

6.
$$\begin{array}{r} 14 \\ -9 \\ \hline \end{array}$$

9.
$$\begin{array}{r} 12 \\ -4 \\ \hline \end{array}$$

10.
$$\begin{array}{r} 9 \\ +6 \\ \hline \end{array}$$

11.
$$\begin{array}{r} 8 \\ +6 \\ \hline \end{array}$$

14.
$$\begin{array}{r} 13 \\ -8 \\ \hline \end{array}$$

12.
$$\begin{array}{r} 8 \\ -7 \\ \hline \end{array}$$

13.
$$\begin{array}{r} 10 \\ -3 \\ \hline \end{array}$$

15.
$$\begin{array}{r} 11 \\ -5 \\ \hline \end{array}$$

Color Code

= 14   Color yellow
< 14   Color blue
> 14   Color red

Name _____

Addition & Subtraction Facts through 20

Gerbils in the Gym

The gerbils try out everything in the gym.

They balance on the beam and swing from the rings.

They tumble on the mat and swing on the bars.

Count the number of gerbils at each place in the gym.

Write number sentences to solve the gerbil problems.

gerbils on the beam + gerbils on the rings = 9

6 + 3 = 9

rings

beam

mat

bars

1. bars + mat = ☐
   ☐ + ☐ = ☐

3. bars + beam = ☐
   ☐ + ☐ = ☐

5. rings + bars = ☐
   ☐ + ☐ = ☐

2. mat + beam = ☐
   ☐ + ☐ = ☐

4. beam – rings = ☐
   ☐ – ☐ = ☐

6. mat – rings = ☐
   ☐ – ☐ = ☐

Name _____

Number Sentences that Match Models

The Sardine Squeeze

So many sardines have come to watch the underwater ball game!
Will they all fit in the ballpark?
Write a number sentence to match each sardine fact below.

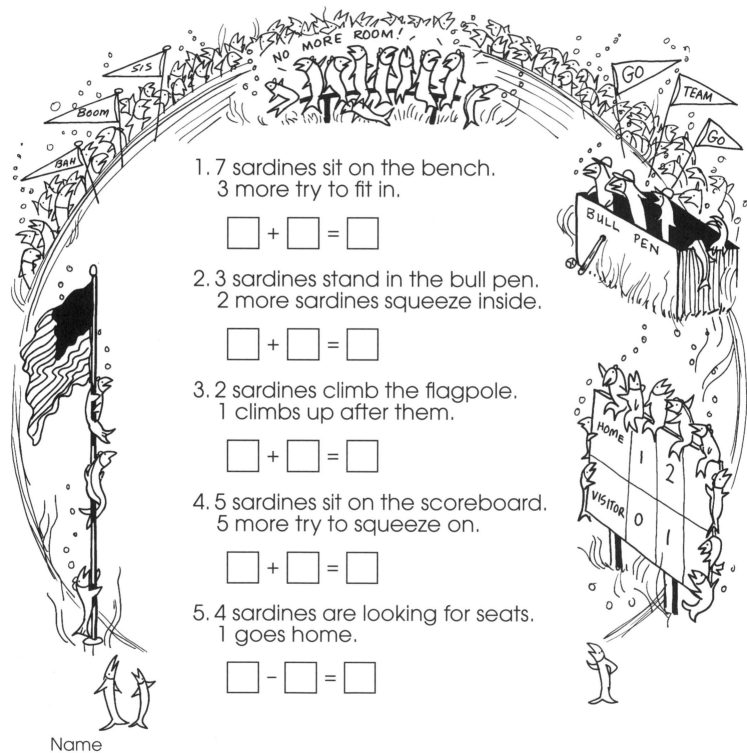

1. 7 sardines sit on the bench.
3 more try to fit in.

☐ + ☐ = ☐

2. 3 sardines stand in the bull pen.
2 more sardines squeeze inside.

☐ + ☐ = ☐

3. 2 sardines climb the flagpole.
1 climbs up after them.

☐ + ☐ = ☐

4. 5 sardines sit on the scoreboard.
5 more try to squeeze on.

☐ + ☐ = ☐

5. 4 sardines are looking for seats.
1 goes home.

☐ – ☐ = ☐

Name _____

Number Sentences that Match Models

10 Pin Math

When Rosie goes bowling, she wants to knock down all 10 pins.

Look at her scorecard to see how she is doing.

Fill in the missing numbers on her scorecard.

Scorecard

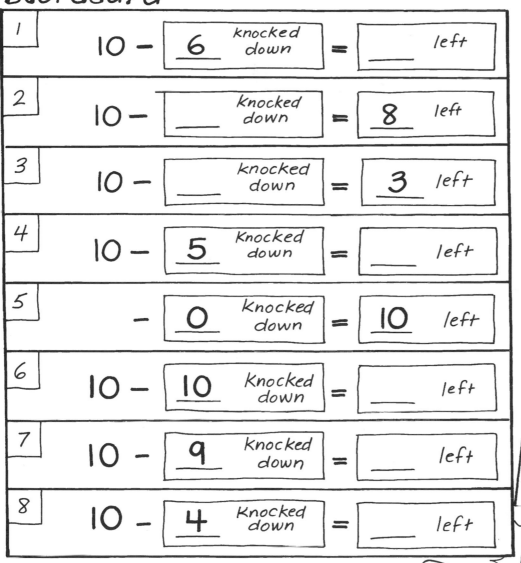

		knocked down		left
1	10 −	6	=	_____
2	10 −	_____	=	8
3	10 −	_____	=	3
4	10 −	5	=	_____
5	−	0	=	10
6	10 −	10	=	_____
7	10 −	9	=	_____
8	10 −	4	=	_____

Name _____

Find Missing Numbers

Turtle Bridges

The turtles are such good friends to the little mice!
They are building bridges to help the mice cross the river.
Write the missing numbers on the turtle bridges.

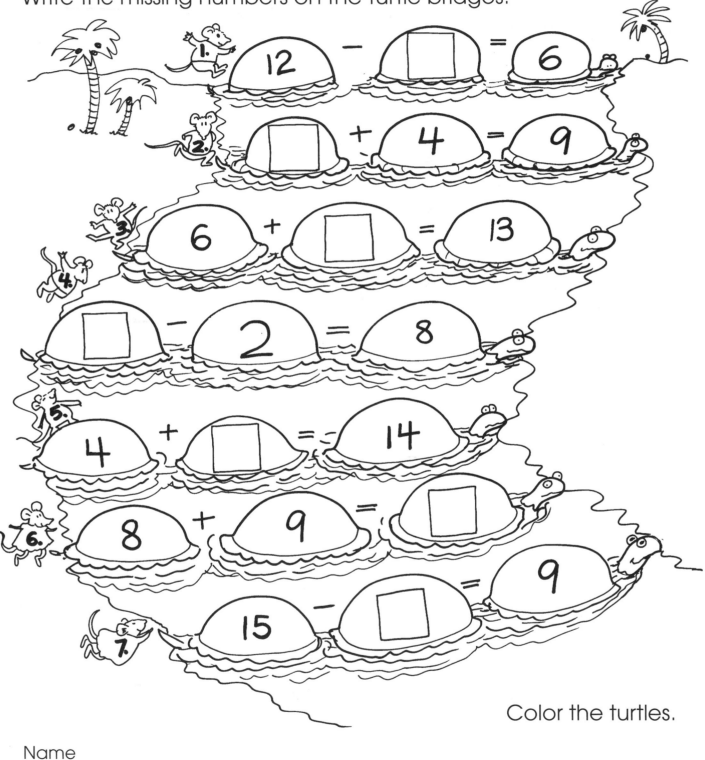

Color the turtles.

Name _____

Find Missing Numbers

Nothing to Do

Zak found Zeke sitting in a mud hole with nothing to do.
Zero is a number that means nothing.

> When you add or subtract 0, the number stays the same.
> $6 + 0 = 6$ $\qquad\qquad$ $6 - 0 = 6$

What are you doing ?

Nothing.

What are you going to do tomorrow.?

The same thing.

Write the answers to these zero problems.

1. 1	2. 10	3. 100	4. 9	5. 99	6. 999	7. 1,000	8. 1,000
+0	+0	+0	−0	−0	−0	+0	−0

9. $0 - 0 =$ ☐   11. Zero − Zero = ☐

10. $0 + 0 =$ ☐   12. Zero + Zero = ☐

Name _____

Add & Subtract with Zero

The Race of the Swamp Serpents

Which serpent will win the big race?
The winner is the serpent with the largest sum.
Add all 3 numbers on each serpent to find the sums.

The winner is
_____
_____

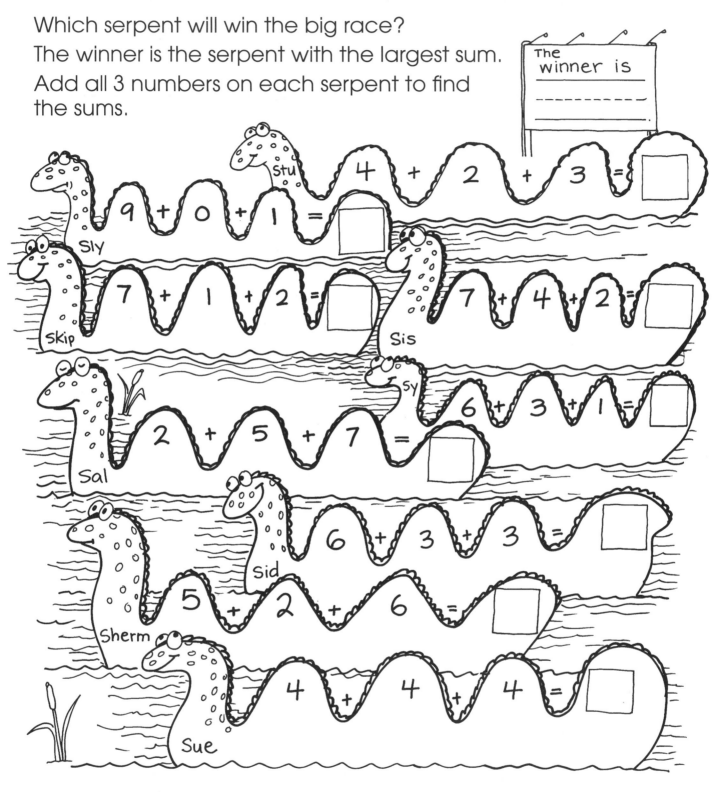

Stu: 4 + 2 + 3 = ☐

Sly: 9 + 0 + 1 = ☐

Skip: 7 + 1 + 2 = ☐

Sis: 7 + 4 + 2 = ☐

Sal: 2 + 5 + 7 = ☐

Sy: 6 + 3 + 1 = ☐

Sid: 6 + 3 + 3 = ☐

Sherm: 5 + 2 + 6 = ☐

Sue: 4 + 4 + 4 = ☐

Color the winner. Write his or her name on the sign.

Name _____

Add 3 Numbers

Mystery on Ice

Buzz and Fuzz think they can win the ice-carving contest.
What are they carving?
Find the answers to the problems.
Follow the **Color Code** to color the spaces.
Then you'll see what they are carving!

Color Code

Answers > 10 = yellow
Answers < 10 = blue

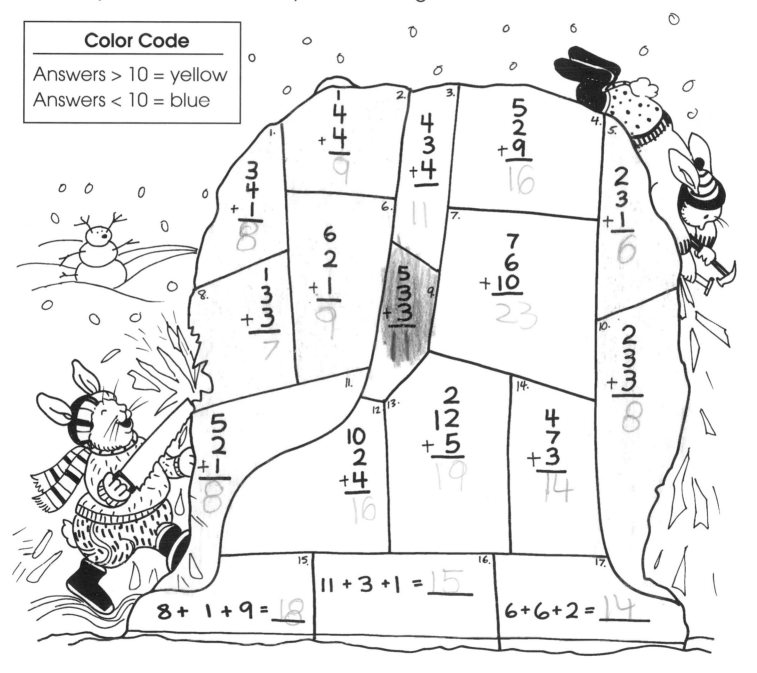

$$1 + 4 + 4 = 9$$
$$4 + 3 + 4 = 11$$
$$5 + 2 + 9 = 16$$
$$3 + 4 + 1 = 8$$
$$2 + 3 + 1 = 6$$
$$6 + 2 + 1 = 9$$
$$5 + 3 + 3 = $$
$$7 + 6 + 10 = 23$$
$$1 + 3 + 3 = 7$$
$$2 + 3 + 3 = 8$$
$$5 + 2 + 1 = 8$$
$$10 + 2 + 4 = 16$$
$$2 + 12 + 5 = 19$$
$$4 + 7 + 3 = 14$$
$$8 + 1 + 9 = 18$$
$$11 + 3 + 1 = 15$$
$$6 + 6 + 2 = 14$$

Name _____

Add 3 Numbers

Checker Problems

Spike is teaching Zip how to play checkers.
He is telling Zip what to do with the checkers.
In math problems, the signs tell you what to do with the numbers.
The signs are missing from all these problems.
You need to put them back!

+ says add.
− says subtract.

Write **+** or **−** in each .

A	14 − 5 = 9						
B	3 + 7 = 10		**G**	11 − 5 = 6			
			H	18 − 9 = 9			
C	15 + 1 = 16		**I**	16 − 9 = 7			
D	8 + 7 = 15		**J**	6 + 7 = 13			
E	4 + 6 = 10		**K**	8 − 4 = 4			
F	13 − 6 = 7						

Name _____

Choose Correct Operation

Bubbles to Juggle

Did you ever see seals juggle?
These seals juggle sea bubbles for fun!
They also count and add the bubbles as they play.
Solve these bubble problems.

Write each answer in the bubble.

1.
$$17 + 2$$

2.
$$26 + 1$$

3.
$$66 + 22$$

4.
$$90 + 6$$

5.
$$37 + 2$$

6.
$$44 + 5$$

7.
$$92 + 4$$

8.
$$15 + 51$$

Color the bubbles blue.
Color the rest of the picture, too!

Name _____

Add 2-Digit Numbers

T-Shirts for T-Ball

These little frogs forgot the name of their T-ball team!
Help them remember by finding the answers to the
T-shirt problems.

Each answer matches a letter in the **Code Box.**

Write the letter on the shirt.

Then read the name of the team.

Code Box
23 = S
38 = G
28 = F
41 = L
66 = E
73 = O
79 = T
85 = R
29 = H

1.
$$68 + 11 = 79$$
T

2.
$$26 + 3$$

3.
$$44 + 22$$

4.
$$15 + 13$$

5.
$$53 + 32$$

6.
$$32 + 41$$

7.
$$16 + 22$$

8.
$$31 + 10$$

9.
$$53 + 13$$

10.
$$14 + 24$$

11.
$$11 + 12$$

What is the name of the team? _____

Name _____

Add 2-Digit Numbers

Look Out Below!

Look out for the snowbank!
The bobsled is headed straight for the snowbank.
Solve all the problems to stop the sled before it crashes!

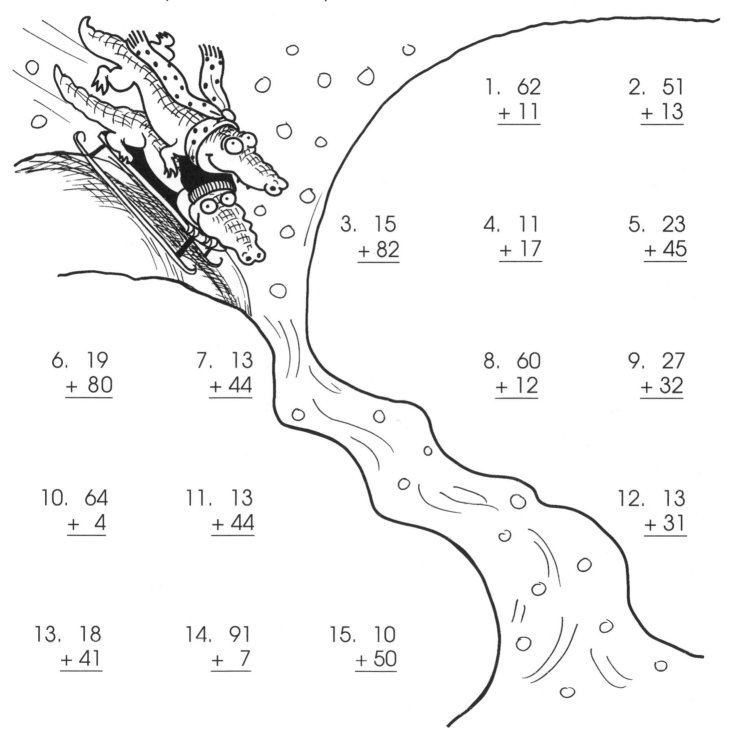

1. 62
    + 11

2. 51
    + 13

3. 15
    + 82

4. 11
    + 17

5. 23
    + 45

6. 19
    + 80

7. 13
    + 44

8. 60
    + 12

9. 27
    + 32

10. 64
    + 4

11. 13
    + 44

12. 13
    + 31

13. 18
    + 41

14. 91
    + 7

15. 10
    + 50

Name _____

Add 2-Digit Numbers

Smashing Fun

Some swamp critters are playing a smashing game of croquet. Find the answers to the problems on the croquet balls. Then follow the **Color Code** to color the balls.

Color Code

Fig is 13. Color each 13 ball green.
Mingo is 14. Color each 14 ball orange.
Di is 15. Color each 15 ball blue.
Tut is 16. Color each 16 ball purple.

1. $25 - 12$

2. $25 - 10$

3. $17 - 1$

4. $46 - 30$

5. $16 - 2$

6. $19 - 3$

7. $15 - 2$

8. $28 - 14$

9. $29 - 14$

10. $36 - 20$

11. $19 - 6$

Color the critter who smashed the most balls.

Name _____

Subtract 2-Digit Numbers

Skating Figure Eights

Cindy Lou and Cy love to skate.

When they skate, they make a lot of eights on the ice.

Solve all the problems.

Check the answers for eights.

How many eights did you find? ☐

$$
\begin{array}{ll}
1.\ \ 12 & 2.\ \ 13 \\
\underline{-\ \ 4} & \underline{-\ \ 2}
\end{array}
$$

$$
\begin{array}{ll}
3.\ \ 19 & 4.\ \ 46 \\
\underline{-\ 11} & \underline{-\ 12}
\end{array}
$$

$$
\begin{array}{ll}
5.\ \ 55 & 6.\ \ 17 \\
\underline{-\ 25} & \underline{+\ 40}
\end{array}
$$

$$
\begin{array}{ll}
7.\ \ 21 & 8.\ \ 18 \\
\underline{+\ \ 5} & \underline{-\ 10}
\end{array}
$$

$$
\begin{array}{ll}
9.\ \ 10 & 10.\ \ 68 \\
\underline{+\ 50} & \underline{-\ 60}
\end{array}
$$

$$
\begin{array}{ll}
11.\ \ 15 & 12.\ \ 55 \\
\underline{+\ 11} & \underline{-\ 22}
\end{array}
$$

$$
\begin{array}{ll}
13.\ \ 18 & 14.\ \ 72 \\
\underline{+\ 11} & \underline{+\ 20}
\end{array}
$$

$$
\begin{array}{ll}
15.\ \ 22 & 16.\ \ 28 \\
\underline{-\ 11} & \underline{-\ 10}
\end{array}
$$

Name _____

Add & Subtract 2-Digit Numbers

Tug-of-War

Tug and pull! Pull and tug!
Who will end up in the mud puddle?
Find the answer to each problem.
Then draw a line to the right answer
on one of the shirts.

1. 12
    + 10

2.   3
    + 10

3. 37
    + 10

4. 16
    + 10

5. 35
    + 10

6. 23
    + 10

7.   7
    + 10

8. 27
    + 10

9. 10
    + 55

10. 58
    + 10

Which team do you think will
end up in the mud puddle?

_____

Why do you think so?

_____

Name _____

Add Tens

Dinosaur Hopscotch

Play hopscotch with the dinosaurs.
Toss a penny 2 times on the board for each problem.
Add the numbers.
Use the spaces below to find the answers.

30 + 40 = 70

wheeeeetteee

90

80   70

60

50   40

30

20

10

1. __30__ + __40__ = __70__

2. _____ + _____ = _____

3. _____ + _____ = _____

4. _____ + _____ = _____

5. _____ + _____ = _____

6. _____ + _____ = _____

Name _____

Add Multiples of Ten

The Alligator Races

Cheer for your favorite alligator team!

The swamp critters are watching the alligator races.

Find the answers to the problems on the umbrellas. Then color the umbrellas by following the **Color Code.**

Color Code

10 = yellow
20 = orange
30 = blue
40 = green

Team 2

$$40 - 20$$ $$60 - 30$$

$$50 - 20$$ $$60 - 40$$

Team 1

$$20 - 10$$ $$50 - 10$$

$$60 - 20$$ $$30 - 20$$

Team 3

$$70 - 60$$ $$30 - 10$$

$$50 - 20$$ $$80 - 40$$

Team 1 colors are _____

Team 2 colors are _____

Team 3 colors are _____

Name _____

Subtract Multiples of Ten

Copyright © 2016 World Book, Inc./
Incentive Publications, Chicago, IL

Happy Hedgehogs

After the badminton game, the hedgehogs went to the Swamp Shack for snacks.

They were happy to find so many tasty treats.

Write a number sentence to show how much money each hedgehog spent.

Gummy Worms 10¢

Candy Crickets 2¢

Taffy Beetles 3¢

Chocolate Ants 5¢

Hank
◻ ¢ + ◻ = ◻ ¢

Haley
◻ ¢ + ◻ = ◻ ¢

Hattie
◻ ¢ + ◻ = ◻ ¢

Hal
◻ ¢ + ◻ = ◻ ¢

Harry
◻ ¢ + ◻ = ◻ ¢

Name _____

Problem Solving with Money

A Mouse in a Machine

The little mice love the new pinball machine.
They like it because it looks like a mouse!
Moe the mouse is made of coins.
Every time the mice play the game, the balls hit different coins.
Use the picture on page 297 to solve these money problems.

Write or circle the correct answer.

1. Moe's ears are worth ☐ ¢ together.

2. Moe's eyes are worth ☐ ¢ together.

3. Which is worth more?
   (Circle one.)

   Moe's eyes   **Moe's arms**

4. Each of Moe's legs is worth ☐ ¢.

5. Moe's tummy is worth ☐ ¢.

Circle > for greater than or < for less than.

6. Moe's eyes + ears   >   < $ 1.00

7. Moe's 2 arms + nose   >   < $ 1.00

8. Moe's legs + eyes   >   < $ 1.00

9. Moe's ears + nose   >   < $ 1.00

10. Moe's tummy + arms   >   < $ 1.00

Name _____

Problem Solving with Money

Use this picture to help you solve the problems on page 296.

Name _____

Use with page 296.

Problem Solving with Money

Join the Rat Race

Help these three fast rats get through the money maze!

For each rat, draw a path from coin to coin.

Use a different color for each path.

Add up the money on each path. Write the total on the finish line.

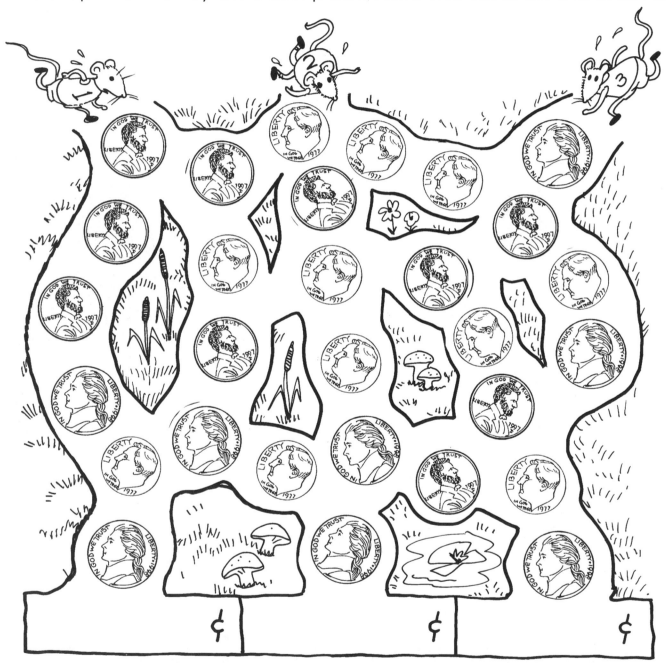

Send the rats through the maze again. Find new paths this time!

Name _____

Problem Solving with Money

Hold Your Breath!

It's hard to hold your breath for a long time underwater! These three friends are having a contest to see which one can hold her breath the longest.

Help Freddy Fish mark their times on the timeline.

1. Draw a pink dot on the timeline for flamingo's time.

2. Draw a green dot for turtle's time.

3. Draw a blue dot for whale's time.

4. Color the animal that can hold its breath the longest blue.

5. Color the animal that needs to breathe most often pink.

Name _____

Cycle Time

Time is so important in a bicycle race!
These riders need your help to keep the time.
Draw the hands on each clock to show the right time.

The race begins at 8 o'clock.

Oh, boy! I won!

The winner crosses the finish line at 10:30.

The last cyclist finishes at 11:00.

1. How long did it take the fastest rider to finish? (Circle one.)
2 hours   2½ hours   3 hours

2. How long did the slowest rider take? (Circle one.)
½ hour   1 hour   3 hours

Name _____

Problem Solving with Time

Friends on Wheels

It's a good afternoon for being out on wheels.
Amy and Alex are doing their favorite sports on Crocodile Lane.
Answer the questions about their time on wheels.

Alex went riding at 10 o'clock.
He rode for 2 hours.
What time did he stop?
_____ o'clock

Then he rode for 1 more hour.
What time did he finish?
_____ o'clock

He rested 1 hour.
What time was it then?
_____ o'clock

Amy went skating at 4 o'clock.
She skated for 1 hour.
What time did she stop?
_____ o'clock

Then she rested for 1 hour.
What time was it then?
_____ o'clock

Then she skated for 1 more hour.
What time did she finish?
_____ o'clock

Alex and Amy were on the same road. Did they meet? **yes   no**

Name _____

Problem Solving with Time

A Full Calendar

What day is soccer practice?

Sam has very busy days.

Just look at his calendar on the next page (page 303).

He plays soccer many days in September.

There are lots of other things to do, too!

Fill in the missing dates on the calendar.

Then follow the directions and answer the questions.

1. Count the number of Tuesdays in this month. ☐

2. How many days are between Monday and Friday? ☐

3. Sam has a soccer game every Saturday. Draw ⚽ on those days.

4. Sam visits his grandma on September 25. Draw a ☺ on that day.

5. Sam will wash his dad's car on the first Saturday. What will the date be?

6. Sam goes swimming on September 11. What day is that?

7. School starts on September 8. What day is that?

8. What is the date of his mom's birthday?

Name _____

Problem Solving with Time

Write the missing dates on the calendar.

SEPTEMBER

Sunday	Monday	Tuesday	Wednesday	Thursday	Friday	Saturday
		1	2			Swamp Town Picnic
6 Soccer practice at 3:30 Cattail Field		First day of Critter School	9	10	One last swim in the mud hole ☹	12
Go to the sea Serpent Races!! 5:00 P.M.	Soccer	15	16	Mom's Birthday (It's a surprise!) Shhhh		19 Clean up the den.
20 Whole family goes to the Daredevil Bat Show. oh, boy!	Soccer	22	23	Bowling with Pee Wee 7:00		
	Soccer	School Field Trip to the Tar Pits. (great)	30 The last day of the month.			

Sam's birthday is on September 6.

Draw a 🎂 on that day.

Name _____

Copyright © 2016 World Book, Inc./
Incentive Publications, Chicago, IL

Problem Solving with Time

Weather Watch

The dinosaurs wanted warm, sunny weather for their Dino Olympics.
What kind of weather did they have?

Weather Chart

Kinds of Weather	NUMBER OF DAYS	1	2	3	4	5	6	7	8
1. Rainy		▓	▓	▓	▓				
2. Sunny		▓	▓	▓	▓	▓	▓	▓	
3. Windy		▓	▓	▓	▓	▓	▓		
4. Cloudy		▓	▓	▓					
5. Cold		▓	▓						

They made a graph of the weather for all the days.
Read the graph to see what the weather was like.
Answer the questions.

1. How many days were rainy? ☐

2. How many days were sunny? ☐

3. How many days were windy? ☐

4. How many days were cloudy? ☐

5. Were there more cold or rainy days? (Circle one.) **cold**   **rainy**

_____

6. Which kind of weather happened most often? - - - - - - - - - - - - - - - - -

_____

Name _____

Problem Solving with a Graph

Horsing Around

It's time for the horseshoe contest! Each game has 2 players.
Peanut has been the champion for 2 years.
Will she win today?
Circle the winner in each game.

score

Game One	
Peanut	21
Smoky	14

Game Two	
Silver	16
Flash	21

Game Three	
Thunder	21
Lightning	11

score

Game Four	
Peanut	21
Thunder	12

Game Five	
Flash	18
Smoky	21

Game Six	
Lightning	21
Silver	19

1. What was the lowest score? ☐

2. How many games did Lightning win? ☐

3. How many games did Silver win? ☐

4. The animal that won the most games is the champion.
   Is Peanut still the champion?   **yes**   **no**

Name _____

Problem Solving with a Chart

Keeping Score

The Stompers were sure their team would win the big game.
The Mashers were sure their team would win the big game.
Now the game is over.
Read the scoreboard to see how each team did in the game.

Quarters	Stompers	Mashers
1st quarter	7	7
2nd quarter	10	7
3rd quarter	16	10
4th quarter	16	17

Circle the correct answer.

1. The Stompers were ahead in the   **1st & 2nd**   **2nd & 3rd** quarters.

2. The teams were tied in the   **1st, 2nd**   **3rd** quarter.

3. The Mashers were ahead in the   **1st, 3rd**   **4th** quarter.

4. The Stompers' score was the same in the
   1st & 3rd   **3rd & 4th** quarters.

5. The winning team was _____ .

Name _____

Problem Solving with a Chart

The Fly Ball

Over the fence comes the ball!
Someone hit a home run at the ball field.
The ball went flying over the fence into the park.
Use the picture to help find the ball.
Answer the questions about the park.

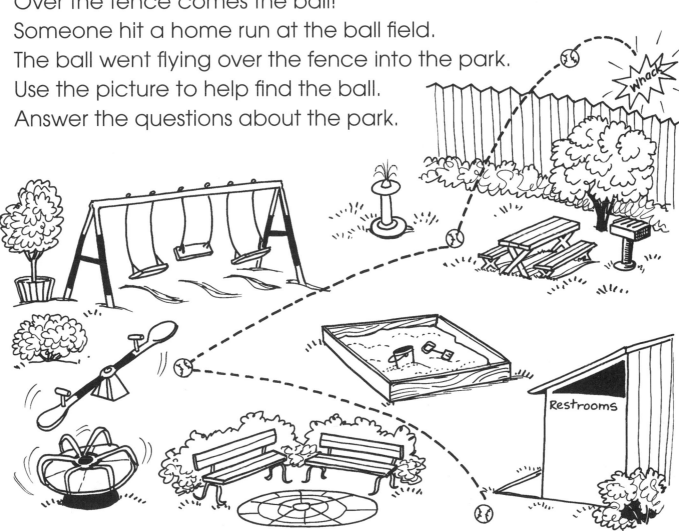

Circle the correct answer.

1. The ball's first bounce is near the **swings**   **picnic table**   **sandbox**

2. Which is closest to the fence?
   benches   **restrooms**   **drinking fountain**

3. The ball's second bounce is near the
   fence   **merry-go-round**   **teeter-totter**

4. The swings are closest to the **sandbox**   **benches**   **restrooms**

5. The ball has stopped near the **swings**   **tree**   **restrooms**

Name _____

Problem Solving with an Illustration

The Sports Lover

Bookworm is just crazy about sports books.
He can't stop reading!
Answer each question about his book reading habit.
Write a problem to help you find each answer.

1. He read 2 books on Monday and 4 books on Tuesday. How many books did he read on those 2 days?

   ☐ + ☐ = ☐

2. On Wednesday he read 5 books. On Thursday he read 6 more. How many books did he read on those 2 days?

   ☐ + ☐ = ☐

3. On Friday he piled up the books he read all week. How many were in the pile?

   ☐ + ☐ = ☐

4. On Saturday, he counted all the books he owned. He had 27. He gave away 5 books. How many did he have left?

   ☐ − ☐ = ☐

Bookworm read his pile of books twice.
Then he ate them!

Name _____

Reading about sports is my favorite sport.

Word Problems

Spring Cleaning

Pack Rat, why are you throwing away all this great stuff?
Look at everything Pack Rat found when he cleaned his room.
Read the sentences below.

Write a number sentence for each one,
and find the answer.

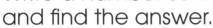

1. He found a baseball bat and a glove.

   1 + 1 = 2

2. He found a snorkel and 2 swim fins.

   ☐ + ☐ = ☐

3. He found a basketball and 2 soccer balls.

   ☐ + ☐ = ☐

4. He found 2 rollerblades, a
   skateboard, and a helmet.

   ☐ + ☐ + ☐ = ☐

5. He found a crazy hat and a baseball.

   ☐ + ☐ = ☐

Name _____

Word Problems

A Wild River Ride

Hang on tight!

The water is moving fast!

Someone has fallen off the raft!

Write number sentences to solve all the problems about the wild river ride.

1. The raft had 5 riders. 1 fell off. How many are left?

2. The friends built the raft in 4 days. They painted it for 2 days. How long did it take to get the raft ready?

3. The animals rode the raft for 2 hours. Then they had a picnic for 1 hour. How long were they together?

4. The friends took 2 raft trips on Monday. They took 1 raft trip on Tuesday. They took 3 raft trips on Wednesday. How many raft trips did they take?

Name _____

Word Problems

Spinning Problems

The merry-go-round makes these friends dizzy.

Play a spinning game that won't get you dizzy!

Make a spinner with a paper clip and your pencil.

See the picture at the top of the page.

Spin the paper clip with your finger.

Watch where it stops.

Spin the paper clip 3 times to get 3 numbers.

Make a problem with the numbers.

Use + or – or both!

Sample: 8 + 4 – 2 = 10

Keep spinning to make 4 problems.

1. _____   3. _____

2. _____   4. _____

Name _____

Create Problems

Two-Point Hoops

Fritz and Fran are shooting hoops.
You and a friend can play, too.
Put this paper on a desk in front of you.
Take turns tossing the penny into the net.
Each of you should toss the penny 5 times.
Score 2 points for each basket.
Score 0 points for
each miss.

Your Score

1 _____

2 _____

3 _____

4 _____

5 _____

Total _____

Friend's Score

1 _____

2 _____

3 _____

4 _____

5 _____

Total _____

What would your score be if you never missed? _____

_____

_____

Explain how you solved this problem. _____

_____

_____

_____

Name _____

Explain Solutions to Problems

High-Jumping Jumpers

All of these animals are prize-winning jumpers.

Who jumped the highest today?

Read all the clues.

Then tell who jumped the highest.

<table>
<tr><th>CLUES</th></tr>
</table>

CLUES

Cricket jumps higher than rabbit.

Rabbit does not jump as high as frog.

Frog does not jump as high as cricket.

Who jumps the highest? _____

Explain how you got your answer. _____

_____

_____

_____

_____

_____

Name _____

Using Logic to Solve Problems

APPENDIX

CONTENTS

Language Arts Skills Test

You will need crayons or markers for parts of this test.

PART ONE: PHONICS & WORD RECOGNITION

Write the **beginning** sound for each picture.

1. _____
2. _____
3. _____

4. _____
5. _____
6. _____

Write the **ending** sound for each picture.

7. _____
8. _____
9. _____

10. _____
11. _____
12. _____

13. Circle all the words that have a **short a** sound, as in hat.

    bake   cape   clap   ape   flag   maid

14. Circle all the words that have a **short i** sound, as in sit.

    bike   tip   lid   pie   dig   six

15. Circle all the words that have a **short o** sound, as in pot.

    hot   rope   boat   home   top   rod

16. Circle all the words that have a **short u** sound, as in tub.

    fun   mud   cube   cut   bug   cute

17. Circle all the words that have a **long e** sound, as in beet.

    pet   keep   feet   beat   read   leg

18. Circle all the words that have a **long i** sound, as in kite.

    bike   ride   zip   nine   pig   lid

19. Circle words where the **y** has a **long e** sound, as in key.

    my   puppy   fry   shy   baby

Name _____

Language Arts Skills Test

Circle the correct **ending** sound for each picture.

20. ch ck st

21. sh ch st

22. st ng nt

23. nd th ng

24. mp nt ng

25. ch th sh

Circle the correct **beginning** sound for each picture.

26. th ch tr

27. th wh sh

28. wh sh ch

29. br bl dr

30. gr fr fl

31. dr br cr

32. Circle the pictures of things that end with a **silent e.**

33. Circle all the naming words.

the   baby   bag   store   was   city   hard

34. Circle the plural nouns.

frogs   water   skates   bees   train   cookies

35. Write the contraction for **do not.** _____

36. Circle the things that rhyme with **fox.**

37. Circle the things that rhyme with **goat.**

Name _____

Copyright © 2016 World Book, Inc./
Incentive Publications, Chicago, IL

38. Number the sentences from 1 to 4 to show the right order.

___ Abby took a big bite.

___ She threw the peach away.

___ She found a fat worm inside.

___ Abby bought a big, juicy peach.

39. Put an **X** beside the best title for this picture.

___ Lightning Strikes the Town

___ The Rain Is Falling   ___ Loud Thunder

___ Under the Umbrella

40. Draw lines to match the words that are **opposites.**

cool   inside   top   slow   start   new

end   bottom   outside   warm   fast   old

41. Draw lines to match the words that mean the **same**.

quick   small   big   angry   wet   scared

frightened   damp   fast   little   mad   large

Look at the picture.

Circle the best answers.

42. Who is wearing a dress?   **Amy   Flo**

43. Is Amy third in line?   **yes   no**

44. Who is second in line?   **Jay   Ned   Flo   Amy**

45. Who is wearing a striped shirt?   **Amy   Flo   Ned   Jay**

Name _____

Language Arts Skills Test

46. Put an **X** in front of the sentence that matches the picture.
   The lion is biting the mouse.
   The mouse is crawling on the lion.
   The mouse is bringing food to the lion.
   The lion is bringing food to the mouse.

47. Follow the directions.
   Draw a hat on the bear.
   Color the bear's skis red.
   Put an X on the bear's nose.
   Draw a snowman next to the bear.

Circle the correct word for each space in the sentence.

48. James **(wanted   went)** to go to the circus.

49. His mom **(said   sad)**, "Let's go!"

50. He **(liked   looked)** seeing the clowns.

51. The clowns did **(sorry   silly)** tricks.

52. James wanted to **(read   ride)** on the elephant.

53. It was **(every   very)** exciting!

Read the story. Then answer the questions.

Sirens are screaming! A fire is burning!
There is smoke everywhere.
Someone in the house cries, "Help!"
The fire engines are going to the fire.
Four firefighters climb their ladders.
They spray water onto the fire.
At last, the fire is out!

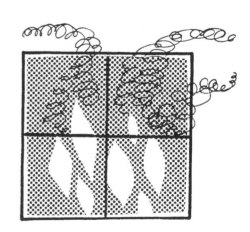

54. Circle the word that means "shouts."

55. How many firefighters climbed ladders? _____

Name _____

Language Arts Skills Test

56. Which thing happened before the fire engines came? Circle it.

The fire was put out.

The firefighters sprayed water on the fire.

The fire started burning.

Read the poem. Then answer the questions.

Tiger's stripes
Are big and bold.
Angelfish has
Stripes of gold.
Raccoon's stripes
Are on his tail.
Zebra looks like
A horse in jail.

57. How many animals are mentioned?

58. What is the same about all the animals? Put an **X** by it.

☐ They are all small.

☐ They all have stripes.

☐ They all swim in the ocean.

59. Put an **X** on the color word in the poem.

60. Circle the word that names a body part.

61. What do you think makes the zebra look like a horse in jail?

_____

- -

_____

62. A good title for this poem would be:

_____

- -

_____

Name _____

Language Arts Skills Test

You will need crayons or markers.

63. Color the balls that have naming words (nouns).

64. Circle the naming words.

    friend   eating   silly   hot   circus   train

65. Circle the words that mean more than one of something.

    tigers   shoe   feet   noses   ride   balloons

66. Circle the proper nouns.

    Florida   fish   Joey   Monday   France   wishes

67. Which groups of words show that someone owns something? Circle the letters.

    A. the clown's nose   C. the elephant's toes

    B. ice cream cones and candy bars   D. Zilla's dog

68. Color the fish that have action words (verbs).

69. Circle the action words (verbs).

    run   happy   tiger   ride   growl   jump

Name _____

Circle the describing words in each sentence.

70. The silly green frog hopped over the little dog.
71. I ate three black jelly beans.
72. Did you ever see such a funny clown?

Write **er** or **est** on the end of the word.

73. My hat is short_____ than yours.
74. Are your feet the long_____ of all the feet?
75. Who is flying high_____ than Flip?
76. Flap is doing the wild_____ tricks of anyone in the circus.

Put a period **(.)** at the end of the **statements** (telling sentences).

Put a question mark **(?)** at the end of the **questions**.

Put an exclamation point **(!)** at the end of the **exclamations**.

77. What an exciting show
78. Which elephant is the biggest
79. We love the lion's roar
80. Don't get too near the tiger
81. Can you buy me some cotton candy

82. Color or shade the signs that have **complete sentences.** Put a capital letter at the beginning and a period at the end of each one.

coming to town

don't miss the circus

watching the parade

you will see funny clowns

wild lions

83. Circle the naming part of this sentence.
    Seven seals balanced balls on their noses.

84. Circle the action part of this sentence.
    Zilla and Lolly fell asleep in the tent.

Name _____

Language Arts Skills Test

85. Circle the words that should have **capital letters.**

africa   thanksgiving   tuesday   animals   july

george   alligator   canada   sister

86. Put **commas** in the right places in the sentence.
The elephants ate peanuts socks carrots gumdrops and cheese.

Circle the **mistakes** in each sentence.

87. rollo and gina Ate four hot Dogs at the circus?

88. let's go see the fire eater Next thursday.

89. how did You like the show !

90. the circus parade went Down main street

91. watch out For the tiger's Teeth

92. Circle every word on the poster that should have a **capital letter.**

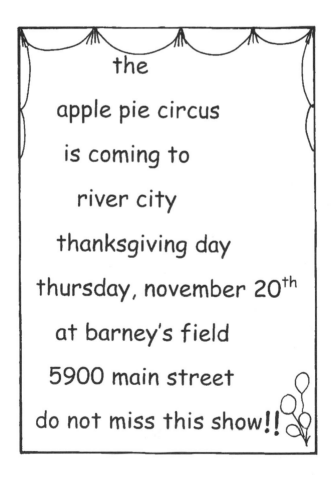

the

apple pie circus

is coming to

river city

thanksgiving day

thursday, november 20th

at barney's field

5900 main street

do not miss this show!!

Name _____

Social Studies Skills Test

PART ONE: SOCIAL STUDIES

CIRCLE THE CORRECT ANSWER.

1. A group of people who live together and care for each other is a

   class   **shelter**   **family**

2. Finding out new things as you grow is called

   learning   **working**   **saving**

3. Some things that tell you what you should or should not do are

   jobs   **rules**   **wants**

4. Some rules help to keep people

   safe   **rich**   **hungry**

5. A place for a person to live and keep warm and safe is a

   job   **club**   **shelter**

6. Food, clothing, shelter, air, water, and love are all

   jobs   **needs**   **goods**

7. Ways people get around are called

   geography   **transportation**   **services**

8. Which picture shows a need?

9. Which picture shows a want, not a need?

10. Texas is a   **state**   **city**   **country**

11. North America is a   **country**   **continent**   **state**

12. The United States is a   **continent**   **state**   **country**

13. Who is the head of the United States?   **queen**   **president**   **mayor**

14. Which one is a symbol for the United States?

15. Which continent is South America?

Name _____

Social Studies Skills Test

16. Where do all people live? **on Earth**   **in America**   **on the ocean**

17. Which is true of all families around the world?

    a. They all live in the same kinds of houses.

    b. They all need food, clothing, shelter, air, water, and love.

    c. They all eat the same kinds of food.

DRAW A LINE TO MATCH EACH PICTURE WITH THE WORD THAT NAMES IT.

18.   island

19.   continent

20.   shelter

21.   flag

22. *WRITE THE DIRECTIONS TO MATCH THE PICTURE. WRITE N FOR NORTH, S FOR SOUTH, E FOR EAST, AND W FOR WEST.*

a. ____

d. ____   b. ____

c. ____

CIRCLE THE CORRECT ANSWER.

23. The symbols on a map are

    pictures   **directions**   **words**

24. George Washington was the first United States

    astronaut   **explorer**   **president**

WRITE THE CORRECT LETTER AND NUMBER THAT TELL WHERE THESE THINGS ARE ON THE GRID.

25. Where is the ⚔ ? _____
26. Where is the 🌴 ? _____
27. Where is the 🐕 ? _____
28. Where is the 🛝 ? _____
29. Where is the ☁ ? _____

Name _____

Social Studies Skills Test

PART TWO: MAP SKILLS & GEOGRAPHY

USE THE MAP AT THE RIGHT TO ANSWER QUESTIONS 30–34.

30. How many houses are on the map? _____

31. How many stores are on the map? _____

32. Is the school on 2nd Street?
    yes   **no**

33. Is the lake near the hospital?
    yes   **no**

34. Is the airport on Main Street?
    yes   **no**

⌂ house   ✈ airport

☐ store   ⊞ hospital

≈ lake   🏫 school

35. Circle the correct map of Maxie's table.

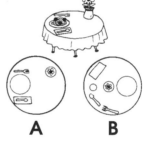

A   **B**

DRAW A LINE TO MATCH EACH WORD TO A SYMBOL.

36.	🌲🌲	campground
37.	⛺	forest
38.	〰	sun
39.	🏠	river
40.	☀	house
41.	💧	fishing
42.	🐟	rain
43.	⊞⊞	railroad

Name _____

Social Studies Skills Test

FOLLOW SARA'S PAW PRINTS ON HER PATH TO ANSWER QUESTIONS 44 –48. WRITE N, S, E, OR W IN EACH BLANK TO TELL WHAT DIRECTION SHE IS WALKING.

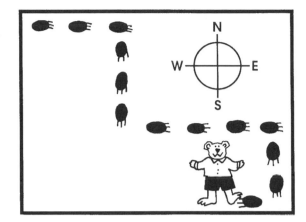

44. Take 3 steps _____ .

45. Take 3 steps _____ .

46. Take 4 steps _____ .

47. Take 2 steps _____ .

48. Take 1 step _____ .

USE THE GRID TO ANSWER QUESTIONS 49–53.

49. Where is the ? _____

50. Where is the ? _____

51. Where is the (HONEY) ? _____

52. Where is the ? _____

53. Where is the ? _____

CIRCLE THE LETTER OF THE CORRECT ANSWER.

54. The map key tells
   A. directions on the map
   B. what the map is about
   C. what symbols mean

55. The map scale tells
   A. directions on the map
   B. what symbols mean
   C. distances on the map

56. The map title tells
   A. what the map is about
   B. distances on the map
   C. what the symbols mean

57. The compass rose shows
   A. what the symbols mean
   B. directions on the map
   C. what the map is about

Name _____

Social Studies Skills Test

*USE THE
WORLD MAP
AT THE RIGHT
TO ANSWER
QUESTIONS 58–60.*

*WRITE THE LETTER
THAT IS ON
EACH PLACE.*

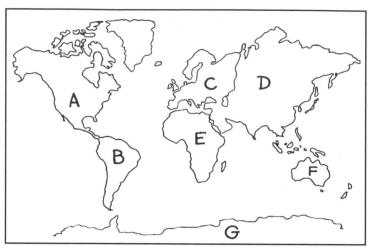

58. North America _____

59. South America _____

60. Africa _____

*USE THE CHART
AT THE RIGHT
TO ANSWER
QUESTIONS 61–65.*

*CIRCLE THE
CORRECT ANSWER.*

Bear Family Jobs

	sweep	wash dishes	feed pets	cook dinner
Morris	X			
Maxie		X		
Noah			X	X

61. Who cooks dinner?   **Noah**   **Maxie**   **Morris**

62. Who has 2 jobs?   **Maxie**   **Noah**   **Morris**

63. Who washes dishes?   **Morris**   **Maxie**   **Noah**

64. What job does Morris do?   **feed pets**   **wash dishes**   **sweep**

65. Does Maxie cook dinner?   **yes**   **no**

*USE THE MAP
AT THE RIGHT
TO ANSWER
QUESTIONS 66–70.*

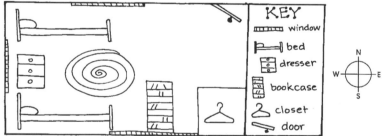

66. How many beds are in the room?   **1**   **2**   **3**

67. How many dressers are in the room?   **1**   **0**   **2**

68. How many windows are in the room?   **1**   **2**   **3**

69. Is the closet south of the door?   **yes**   **no**

70. The bookcase is next to the   **door**   **dresser**   **bed**

Name _____

Social Studies Skills Test

Science Skills Test

CIRCLE THE CORRECT ANSWERS.

1. Which things are alive?

2. Which arrow points to the roots?

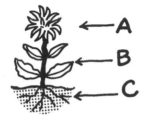

3. Which one comes first?

4. Which animal does not belong in this group?

5. Which animal does not belong in this group?

6. Which bugs are insects?

7. Which animal has fur for a body covering?

8. Which tracks belong to this animal?

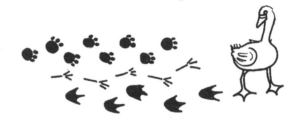

9. Which animal belongs in this home?

10. Which animal belongs in an ocean habitat?

11. Which bone is the skull?

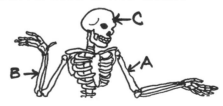

12. Which food is unhealthy?

Name _____

CIRCLE THE CORRECT ANSWER OR ANSWERS.

13. Which plant part makes food?   **roots**   **stem**   **leaves**

14. Which plant part makes seeds?   **stem**   **flower**   **leaves**

15. A fish is covered with _____.   **scales**   **fur**   **feathers**

16. Which animal hops?   **a snake**   **a fish**   **a whale**   **a rabbit**

17. Which body parts can you see from the outside?

   tongue   **teeth**   **heart**   **elbow**   **lungs**

18. Which body system helps you feel things?

   bones   **blood**   **nerves**   **breathing**

19. Earth moves around the _____.   **moon**   **sun**

20. The moon moves around the _____.   **the sun**   **Earth**

MATCH THE BODY PARTS TO THE WORDS.

21. ribs _____

22. ankle _____

23. brain _____

24. lungs _____

25. heart _____

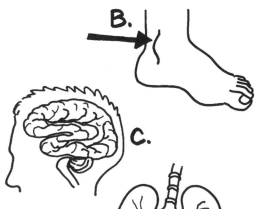
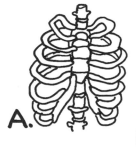

Name _____

CIRCLE THE CORRECT ANSWERS.

26. Which body part is used to hear?

27. Which things are NOT safe?

28. Which one is Earth?

29. Which season is this?

winter   summer   spring   fall

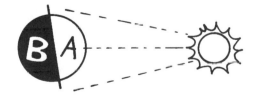

30. Which letter is on the part of Earth where it is night?

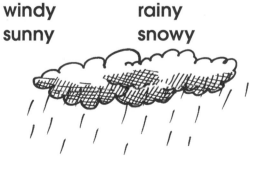

31. Which things are solids?

32. Which things use electricity?

33. Which one of these things is melting?

34. Which things show that air is moving?

35. Which weather is shown here?

windy   rainy
sunny   snowy

Name _____

Science Skills Test

Math Skills Test

PART ONE: NUMBERS & COUNTING

Write a number to match the sets.

1. _____

2. _____

3. Count by twos. Fill in the missing numbers.

2	4		8		12	14	

4. Count by fives. Fill in the missing numbers.

5		15			30		40

5. Count by tens. Fill in the missing numbers.

10			40		60			90	

Name _____

Math Skills Test

Look at the picture below. Circle the right answer.

6. Who is second?   Todd   Joe   Deb

7. Who is fifth?   Ann   Sam   Todd

8. Who is first?   Deb   Bob   Sam

9. Where is Joe?   second   third   fourth

10. Where is Sam?   fourth   fifth   sixth

BOB   DEB   JOE   ANN   TODD   SAM

Write the number for each of these.

11. four tens three ones   ☐   12. six tens seven ones   ☐

13. two tens no ones   ☐   14. eight tens five ones   ☐

Write the number for each word.

15. three ☐   16. zero ☐   17. nine ☐

18. seven ☐   19. twelve ☐   20. thirty ☐

21. eleven ☐   22. sixteen ☐   23. twenty ☐

Name _____

Math Skills Test

24. Circle the biggest number.   33   13   63   316

25. Circle the biggest number.   80   50   20   30   60

26. How much money? _____ ¢   27. How much money? _____ ¢

Write the missing number for each sentence.

28. [   ] = 70 + 7   31. [   ] = 100 + 10 + 1

29. [   ] = 90 + 2   32. [   ] = 70 + 9

30. [   ] = 40 + 8

33. Put a box around the clock that says 5:30.

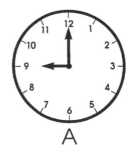   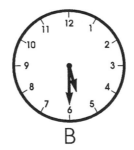   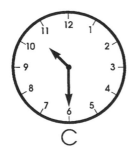

A   B   C

Write the time that each clock shows.

34. 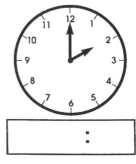   35. 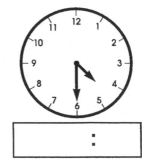   36.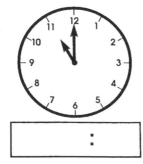

[:   ]   [:   ]   [:   ]

Name _____

Look at the
number line.
Circle the
right answer.

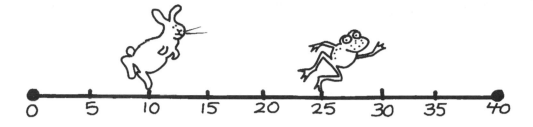

37. Where is the ?   5   10   25   30

38. Where is the ?   5   10   25   30

39. Which picture shows $\frac{2}{3}$ of a pizza left? Put a box around it.

A. 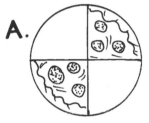   B.    C.

40. Circle the heaviest.

A.    B.    C.

41. Circle the one that holds the most.

A.   B.   C.

Name _____

PART TWO: MATH COMPUTATION & PROBLEM SOLVING

Write the answers.

42. [flowers] + [flowers] = [ ]

43. [ladybugs] − [ladybugs] = [ ]

44. 3 + 3 = [ ]   45. 7 − 2 = [ ]   46. 6 + 4 = [ ]

47. 9 − 6 = [ ]   48. 5 + 5 = [ ]

49. [coin] − [coin] = [ ] ¢

50. [coin] + [coin] + [coin] + [coin] + [coin] + [coin] + [coin] = [ ] ¢

51. 7   52. 9   53. 8   54. 12   55. 5
    + 4   − 5   + 8   − 4   + 8

56. 10   57. 4   58. 10   59. 6   60. 13
    − 7   + 9   − 7   + 2   − 4

Name _____

Write a number sentence to go with each picture.

61.

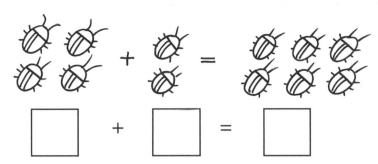

☐ + ☐ = ☐

62.

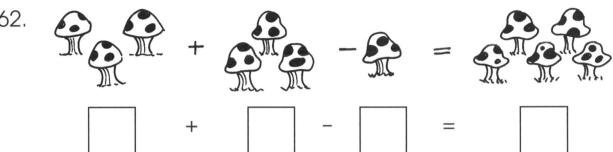

☐ + ☐ – ☐ = ☐

Write the missing numbers.

63. ☐ – 7 = 9   64. 8 + ☐ = 10   65. ☐ – 3 = 6

66. 6 + ☐ = 12   67. ☐ + 3 = 8   68. ☐ + 5 = 11

69. 6 + ☐ = 15   70. ☐ + 9 = 11   71. 17 – ☐ = 10

72. ☐ + 8 = 15

73. What time does the clock show? _____ o'clock

74. What time will it be in 2 hours? _____ o'clock

Name _____

75. 26	76. 49	77. 12	78. 30	79. 66
+ 3	− 23	+ 6	− 20	+ 10

Write the missing signs + or −.

80. 8 ☐ 6 = 14   81. 4 ☐ 3 = 7   82. 12 ☐ 9 = 3

Look at the chart to answer the questions.

83. What was Sid's time? ☐

84. Who was faster than Sly? (Circle one.)
Sal   Sue   Sid

85. Who was the slowest? (Circle one.)
Sal   Sid   Sly   Sue

SEA SERPENT RACES	
SWIMMER	TIME
1. Sly	4 min.
2. Sid	6 min.
3. Sal	7 min.
4. Sue	3 min.

Look at the graph to answer the questions.

86. On which day did Sandy sell the most shells? (Circle one.)

Monday   Tuesday   Wednesday

87. How many shells did Sandy sell on Monday? ☐

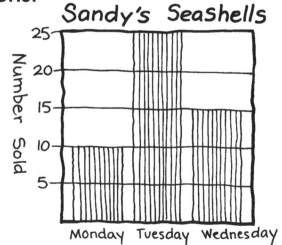

Sandy's Seashells

Name _____

Math Skills Test

Write a problem to find the answers.

88. Dino scored 27 points in the first game.

   He scored 10 points in the second game.

   How many points did he score in all?

89. Mimi fell 12 times on Monday.

   She fell 5 times on Tuesday.

   She fell 2 times on Wednesday.

   How many times did she fall all together?

90. Frog brought 14 candy bars to diving class.

   He gave 7 away.

   How many did he have left?

91. Tom had $35 in his turtle bank.

   He spent $22 on new skates.

   How much money does he have left?

Name _____

Skills Test Answer Key

Language Arts Skills Test

1. b
2. f
3. d
4. h
5. l
6. p
7. d
8. t or p
9. g or d
10. n
11. b
12. k
13. clap, flag
14. tip, lid, dig, six
15. hot, top, rod
16. fun, mud, cut, bug
17. keep, feet, beat, read
18. bike, ride, nine
19. puppy, baby
20. ck
21. sh
22. nt
23. ng
24. mp
25. th
26. th
27. wh
28. ch
29. br
30. fr
31. cr
32. bike, kite
33. baby, bag, store, city
34. frogs, skates, bees, cookies
35. don't
36. socks, box
37. coat, boat
38. 2, 4, 3, 1
39. Lightning Strikes the Town
40. cool—warm
    inside—outside
    top—bottom
    slow—fast
    start—end
    new—old
41. quick—fast
    small—little
    big—large
    angry—mad
    wet—damp scared—
    frightened
42. Amy
43. no
44. Flo

45. Jay
46. The mouse is bringing food to the lion.
47. Review student drawing to see:
    hat on bear,
    skis colored red,
    X on bear's nose,
    snowman drawn next to bear
48. wanted
49. said
50. liked
51. silly
52. ride
53. very
54. cries
55. 4
56. The fire started burning.
57. 4
58. They all have stripes.
59. gold
60. tail
61. The zebra's stripes make him look like he is a horse behind jail bars.
62. Answers will vary. See that title fits poem.
63. Color these balls:
    clown, lion, hat, candy, tiger, ball
64. friend, circus, train
65. tigers, feet, noses, balloons
66. Florida, Joey, Monday, France
67. A, C, D
68. leap, clap, cheer, throw
69. run, ride, growl, jump
70. silly, green, little
71. three, black, jelly
72. funny
73. er
74. est
75. er
76. est
77. !
78. ?
79. .
80. !
81. ?
82. Don't miss the circus. You will see funny clowns.
83. Seven seals
84. fell asleep in the tent
85. Africa, Thanksgiving, Tuesday, July, George, Canada

86. The elephants ate peanuts, socks, carrots, gumdrops, and cheese.
87. Rollo and Gina ate four hot dogs at the circus.
88. Let's go see the fire eater next Thursday.
89. How did you like the show?
90. The circus parade went down Main Street.
91. Watch out for the tiger's teeth!
92. The, Apple, Pie, Circus, River, City, Thanksgiving, Day, Thursday, November, Barney's, Field, Main, Street, Do

Social Studies Skills Test

1. family
2. learning
3. rules
4. safe
5. shelter
6. needs
7. transportation
8. C
9. A
10. state
11. continent
12. country
13. president
14. B
15. A
16. on Earth
17. b
18. flag
19. island
20. continent
21. shelter
22. a. N
    b. E
    c. S
    d. W
23. pictures
24. president
25. B, 3
26. D, 3
27. C, 1
28. D, 1
29. C, 4
30. 7
31. 5
32. no
33. yes
34. yes

35. A
36. forest
37. campground
38. river
39. house
40. sun
41. rain
42. fishing
43. railroad
44. E
45. S
46. E
47. S
48. W
49. B, 3
50. D, 4
51. C, 2
52. B, 1
53. A, 5
54. C
55. C
56. A
57. B
58. A
59. B
60. E
61. Noah
62. Noah
63. Maxie
64. sweep
65. no
66. 2
67. 1
68. 3
69. yes
70. bed

Science Skills Test

1. bird, flower
2. C
3. 1st picture—roots
4. fish
5. prairie dog
6. ant, ladybug
7. mouse
8. bottom tracks
9. beaver
10. octopus
11. C
12. lollipop
13. leaves
14. flower
15. scales
16. a rabbit
17. tongue, teeth, elbow
18. nerves
19. sun
20. Earth
21. A
22. B

23. C
24. E
25. D
26. ear
27. knife, matches, poison
28. body in center
29. winter
30. B
31. stool, bike
32. toaster, TV
33. ice cube
34. blowing hair, tree
35. rainy

Math Skills Test

1. 8
2. 10
3. Missing: 6, 10, 16
4. Missing: 10, 20, 25, 35
5. Missing: 20, 30, 50, 70, 80, 100
6. Deb
7. Todd
8. Bob
9. third
10. sixth
11. 43
12. 67
13. 20
14. 85
15. 3
16. 0
17. 9
18. 7
19. 12
20. 30
21. 11
22. 16
23. 20
24. 316
25. 80
26. 70¢
27. 50¢
28. 77
29. 92
30. 48
31. 111
32. 79
33. B
34. 2:00
35. 4:30
36. 11:00
37. 10
38. 25
39. B
40. B
41. C
42. 7
43. 5
44. 6

45. 5
46. 10
47. 3
48. 10
49. 20¢
50. 56¢
51. 11
52. 4
53. 16
54. 8
55. 13
56. 3
57. 13
58. 3
59. 8
60. 9
61. 4 + 2 = 6
62. 3 + 3 − 1 = 5
63. 16
64. 2
65. 9
66. 6
67. 5
68. 6
69. 9
70. 2
71. 7
72. 7
73. 10
74. 4
75. 29
76. 26
77. 18
78. 10
79. 76
80. +
81. +
82. −
83. 6
84. Sue
85. Sal
86. Tuesday
87. 10

88. 27
   $\underline{+10}$
   37

89. 12
   5
   $\underline{+\ 2}$
   19

90. 14 − 7 = 7

91. $ 35
   $\underline{-\ \$\ 22}$
   $ 13

Skills Test Answer Key

Skills Exercises Answer Key

page 1
See that lines are drawn matching all uppercase to lowercase letters and capital vowels are circled.

page 22
See that student follows ABC order with a colored path and circles all consonants.

page 23
Molly Mouse is sailing a sailboat.

page 24
Path: stop, map, shut, twig, ten, rope, make, fire, sees, star

page 25
Correct coloring reveals a carrot, potatoes, and a beet.

page 26
See that all vowels are colored blue and all consonants are colored red. **Y** may be colored either blue or red.

page 27
Answers may vary, because students may give different labels to things.
Any 3 correct words are acceptable. Possible answers:
B-brown: bird, bear, bunny, bat, bee, bug
F-orange: fox, frog, feet, fire, flowers
S-blue: shoes, socks, snake, stump, squirrel, snow

page 28
The arrangement of the words in the lines may vary.
1. think, thick, thumbs
2. whale, wheels, white, whistle
3. chair, chain, chip, chocolate

page 29
See that students have properly traced letters and colored the pictures:
frogs=green
creek=blue
flowers=red
ground=brown
clouds=gray
rain=blue
grass=pink
Pink is the silly color word.

page 30
1. desert
2. pony
3. shadow
4. tipi
5. flower
6. lizard
7. robin

page 31
1. school
2. sled
3. scarf
4. skates
5. square
6. snowman

page 32
Lines should connect these pictures:
1. train, moon, sun
2. duck, book, clock
3. snail, tail, nail
4. hand, sled, bed

page 33
1. rattle
2. bunny
3. apple
4. puddle

page 34
1. nest
2. clock
3. neck
4. peach
5. hand
6. watch
7. ring
8. match
Ellie is an elephant.

page 35
Hidden pictures with short i: fish, mitten, six, pig, pin
Hidden pictures with short u: sun, nut, cup, skunk, tub

page 36
Drawings in Anna's trunk: apple, hat, fan, map, can
Drawings in Robbie's trunk:
doll, sock, clock, dog

page 37
Roller coaster words:
cake, face, kite, bike, fire

page 38
Things with long vowels: cheese, rose, pie, cake, grapes, plates, knives, pineapple

page 39
Path formed by words: mouse, owl, clown, brown, out, cow, down, cloud, flower, town, house, crown

page 40
Answers will vary somewhat, as different students will notice different things and label some things differently.
Possibilities: leaves, kite, mail, tree, goat, sheep, coat, bee, shoe, side-walk, mailman, bone, light, mice, pole, road

page 41
1. goose
2. sheep
3. moose
4. bee
Quotations chosen from Box 2 will vary.

page 42
1. seal, toast; no
2. eat, boat; no
3 toad, road; yes
4. bee, sleep; no
5. sleep; yes
6. tree, read; no
7. no
8. coat, eat, goat; no

page 43
Yellow balls: pony, pretty,
city, baby, messy, smelly, tiny, scary, bunny, candy
Red balls: buy, try, fry, fly, my, why, cry

page 44
Opposites
Yellow: up—down, tall— short, happy— sad, good—bad, light—dark, noisy— quiet, on—off, old— new, more—less Same
Blue: shut—close, yell— shout, always—forever, small—tiny, begin— start, quiet—hush, friend—pal, loud— noisy, big—large, laugh—giggle, silly— funny

page 45
Check to see that proper pictures have been drawn.

page 46
Students' drawings will vary. Check to see that pictures students have drawn are placed in the appropriate columns.

page 47
1. City Zoo
2. Fish Lake
3. Mark Brown
4. Santa Claus; North Pole
5. Camp Pine Tree

page 48
X's should be on clam, whale, boat, and prize. Check to see that students have written 4 plural nouns on shell.

page 49
I am—I'm
we are—we're
he will—he'll
can not—can't
is not—isn't
she is—she's
have not—haven't

you are—you're
that is—that's
I will—I'll
it is—it's
what is—what's

page 50
Connect these pictures in
the left-hand balloon:
frog-log, frog-dog,
dog-log, man-can,
fan-can, fan-man
Connect these pictures in
the right-hand balloon:
bat-cat, car-star, car-jar,
star-jar, hen-pen

page 51
1. popcorn
2. baseball
3. greenhouse
4. toothbrush

page 52
See that student has
finished each drawing to
match book title.

page 53
1. A Bullfighter in Trouble
2. A Big Tornado
3. Look Out Ahead!
4. A Bear Hangs On

page 54
1. Don't feed the boa!
2. Leaping lizards
   ahead!
3. Stop for tap dancing
   turtles!
4. Look out for smoking
   dragons!
5. Beware of the cross-
   eyed moose!
6. Caterpillar crossing!

page 55
See that student has
drawn lines to the
correct spots on the
picture.

page 56
1. the frog
2. the rabbit
3. the mouse
4. the chicken
5. the duck
6. the spider

page 57
1. C   4. B
2. A   5. D
3. E

page 58
1. an alligator
2. big
3. yes
4. no
5. no
6. the neighbors
7. Answers will vary.

page 59
1. Quill School
2. River
3. Pinpoint
4. Shaky
5. Prickle
6. hole

page 60
1. no   4. no
2. bear   5. moose
3. rattlesnake

page 61
3, 5, 1, 4, 2
1. Dear Goldie,
2. You came to my house.
3. You broke my chair!
4. You ran away!
5. Sadly yours, Baby Bear

page 62
Before: Get a treasure
   map. Find some shovels.
During: Follow the map.
   Dig for the treasure.
After: Take the treasure
   home. Enjoy the treasure.

page 63
3, 6, 1, 4, 5, 2, 7

page 64
Look at student drawings
to see that they have
followed directions
correctly.

page 65
Look at student drawings
to see that they have
followed directions
correctly.

page 66
1. a sailor
2. sea, see
3. the sea, sea, sea
4. Answers may vary (Best
   answer: an octopus).

page 67
1. big
2. green with black spots
3. in the rain forest
4. They squeeze it.

page 68
1. Jack
2. a mouse
3. hat
4. yes
5. Hall or all

page 69
1. arctic fox, arctic hare;
   name, small ears,
   small tail (rabbit)
2. desert fox, jackrabbit;
   big ears, big tail (fox)

page 70
Answers will vary.

page 71
1. sun
2. peek
3. rain
4. blue
5. sea
6. bye
7. Eight
8. Aunt
9. too

page 72
See that student has
colored spaces correctly
to find the letters I, C.

page 73
See that student has
colored spaces correctly
to find the letters M, T.

page 74
The word "Sir" should be
colored in.
Red = huge, enormous
Blue = tiny, dwarf
Yellow = slush, soggy,
   damp
Green = crash, scream,
   siren, whistle, yell, shout
Orange = glad, joyful
Purple = chocolate,
   olive, cabbage,
   pickles, jam, ice cream,
   pudding, beans,
   applesauce, spaghetti,
   yams, onion, corn,
   syrup, beets

page 75
Jack follows these
   words to his desert
   home: hot, burn,
   warm, bake, boil, oven,
   fire, flames, simmer,
   roast, blaze, sizzle,
   desert.

Sam follows these
   words to his cold
   home: arctic, polar,
   zero, chilly, frozen,
   nippy, winter, frosty,
   freeze, icy, cool.

page 76
1. night   4. wind
2. sitting   5. huge
3. scary   6. rabbit

page 77
WET PAINT
STOP
QUIET
FOR SALE
DOGS WALKING
NO PARKING

page 78
Answers will vary.

page 79
Answers will vary.
Check to see that
student has written
something for all
categories on the
list and that
capitalization is
correct.

page 80
Answers will vary.

pages 81–82
Answers will vary.

page 83
Answers will vary.

page 84
Answers will vary.

page 85
Answers will vary.
Check to see that
student has written 1
statement, 1 question,
and 1 exclamation.

page 86
Answers will vary.
Check to see that
student has written
10 reasonable
selections.

page 87
Answers will vary.
Check to see that
student has written
words below each
word shown.

Skills Exercises Answer Key

page 88

Check to see that student has accurately completed the dot-to-dot.

page 89

1. camel
2. lion
3. bear
4. monkey
5. zebra
6. clown

Check to see that student has colored the words in the puzzle.

page 90

See corrected text:

1. Why did the clown throw the clock out the window? She wanted to see time fly. (or !)
2. Why are fish so smart? They are smart because they live in schools. (or !)
3. What do you call a dog at the beach? A hot dog. (or !)
4. Why is 6 afraid of 7? He's afraid because 7 8 9. (or !)
5. Why is 2 + 2 = 5 like your left hand? It's not right. (or !)
6. How did the ocean say good-bye? It waved. (or !)

page 91

See corrected text:

Dear Flip, Flap, and Flop,

Hello! (or .) My name is Happy Frog.
I live in Stinky Swamp! (or .) I love your act! (or .) I want to join the circus. Do you need another brother?

Your friend, Happy

page 92

All sayings have exclamation points.

page 93

See corrected text:

1. Elephants like lots and lots of hay, grass, leaves, fruit, and branches.
2. Chimps get some nuts, leaves, honey, ants, and bananas.
3. Lions eat roast, chops, liver, and bones for their teeth.
4. Seals love things from the sea like fish, eels, squid, and clams.

page 94

Questions are:
1, 2, 3, 4, 7, 8

Answers:
1. yes
2. 25¢
3. yes
4. Lolly
7. no
8. Answers will vary.

page 95

See corrected text:

I look like a skinny guy from outer space. All I need is green skin.
I am so short. I could fit into a mouse's clothes.
I look so wide. I could be a beach ball.
Hey, this is cool. I'm Mighty Mo the super hero.

page 96

See that student has colored the page correctly.

page 97

See corrected text:

Yippee! I am such a lucky guy. I am going to pick roses and pink tulips with my mom today. I think pink is the prettiest color in the world. We are going to go to a tea party, too. Miss Sherry Twinkletoes is giving the party. She is my best friend.

page 98

1. T	6. B
2. O	7. A
3. I	8. M
4. C	9. S
5. I	

Riddle Solution:
IT IS A COMB!

page 99

1. Flying, Fred, Apple, Pie, Circus
2. Paris, France (Some may capitalize Clown Circus also.)
3. Lolly, Miami, Florida
4. Zorba, July, San Francisco
5. Tracy, Stacy, Wednesday

page 100

See corrected addresses:

Sir Tiny Taylor
    300 Blackberry Street
    Bramble, England
Mrs. Jane Hopper
    501 Rye Lane
    Sweet Home, Oregon
Santa Claus
    North Pole
Mr. Lee Chen
    201 Jade Road
    Beijing, China
Mrs. Donna Prima
    412 Main Street
    Toledo, Ohio

return to:
Z. Zucchini
    590 Palm St.
    Winter Park, Florida

page 101

we are—we're
she is—she's
I am—I'm
is not—isn't
can not—can't
will not—won't
does not—doesn't
did not—didn't
I will—I'll

page 102

Answers will vary.
See that student has added an action part to each sentence to make a complete sentence.

page 103

1. Snakes
2. Ants
3. Robert
4. Hippos
5. Holly
5. I
6. Ink

Riddle solution: HIS HAIR

page 104

1. Naming: The rocket blaster. Action: shoots through the air.
2. Naming: The small cars. Action: fly past the twins.
3. Naming part: The toy planes. Action part: buzz around and around.
4. Naming part: The roller coaster. Action part: goes racing by.
5. Naming part: The Ferris wheel. Action part: touches the treetops.
6. Naming part: The painted ponies. Action part: prance up and down.

page 105

1. !
2. !
3. .
4. ?
5. ! or .
6. !
7. !
8. ! or .
9. ?
10. ! or .
11. ! or .
12. ! or .

page 106

Exclamations are:
1, 2, 3, 4, 7, 8

page 107

nouns: fish, seal, eye, ball, tank, sea, water, food

verbs: juggle, jump, throw, flip, catch, swim, eat

describing words: wet, green, slippery, icy, pretty, happy, cold, blue, deep, funny, big

page 108

2. bigger
   shorter
   longer
3. biggest
   shortest
   longest

page 109
1. two, black
2. pink
3. big, red
4. green
5. pretty, happy
Look to see that student has completed the drawings and has colored the pictures.

page 110
1. sew
2. sweep
3. scrub
4. wash
5. paint
6. carry
7. mop

page 111
1. Flip or Flop
2. Flip or Flop
3. Honey Berry
4. Lolly
5. Strong Sam

page 112
people: lady, clown, boy
places: zoo, circus
things: shoe, plate, balloon

page 113
See corrected passage:
Punctuation may vary somewhat. Exclamation points may be interchanged with periods in many places.
Step right up! See the oddest show on Earth!
Look at the pink dinosaur. It eats popcorn for dinner.
See a kitty as big as a moose and a horse as small as a mouse.
I have an ant with two heads. There is a dog with six ears.
Hear my frog sing "Jingle Bells." Watch her dance!
Stare at a snake with arms and legs. See a pig fly!
Watch a flea in pajamas! You will not believe your eyes!
See a creature from outer space! He is goofy!

page 114
Complete sentences are:
I work for peanuts.
This hat is too big.
Let's have some fun.
I like to dress up.
Can you help me?
We look so cute.

page 115
Complete sentences are:
My puppy is lost.
I am so sad.
I want to find him.
He may be hungry.
Here he is now.

page 116
Complete sentences are:
3, 4, 5, 6, 8, 9, 11, 13, 14, 15
Student gives lion 10 teeth.
He has one already, making a total of 11.

page 117
Questions are: 2, 3, 4, 5, 7, 9
Students' ideas about what fizzles are will vary.

page 118
yellow statements:
The moon is shining.
The stars twinkle.
The circus is sleeping.
Stars are bright.
The flags are waving.
All is quiet.
This is the Big Top.
It is nighttime.
All other spaces are blue.

page 119
Yellow Balls (verbs): jump, juggle, run, play, read, swim, hop, walk

page 120
1. Joey's button
2. Alf's hat
3. Zilla's flower
4. Lolly's nose
5. Polly's bow
6. Mick's glove

page 121
Joey—single things: shoe, sock, key, glove, book, pen, hat
Zilla—plural things: shoes, socks, books, gloves, hats, pens, keys

page 122
Nouns on path:
trunk   zucchini
flowers   shoe
nose   lady
circus   tiger

page 123
color: elephants, clowns, acrobats, clown kids, zebras, weights, balloons, wheels

page 124
Nouns on path:
tiger   box
tent   clown
balloon   rose
nose   animal
wheels   cage
cab   truck

page 125
Answers will vary.

pages 130–131
Answers will vary.

page 132
Answers will vary.

page 133
Answers will vary.

page 134
1. 2
2. 4
3. 1
4. 1 and 3

page 135
Answers will vary.

pages 136–137
A. 2   F. 6
B. 4   G. 3 (or 4)
C. 5   H. 7
D. 4   I. 5
E. 2

page 138
See that student answers fit the assignment.

page 139
See that student answers fit the assignment.

page 140
Match the following:
4—a friendship
5—a dance class
6—school
2—a team
1—a club
3—church

page 141
1. 4
2. 1
3. 2
4. Picture 3 should be colored

pages 142–143
1. 220 Bush Street
2. The Steins
3. The Travises and the Habeebs
4. The Steins
5. Maple Street
6. 124 Maple Street

page 144
Maps will vary.

page 145
1. A, 1   5. B, 1
2. C, 1   6. D, 3
3. A, 3   7. B, 3
4. D, 1   8. D, 4

page 146
Answers will vary somewhat. Look at pictures to see that students have circled workers. Possible number: 26 (Student may or may not include biker and people in bus.)

page 147
Answers will vary.

pages 148–149
Answers will vary. See that student has completed all exercises.

page 150
See that student has colored each of the items listed.

page 151
See that student has correctly completed the dot-to-dot and has written the president's name.

page 152
See that student has correctly completed the dot-to-dot.

Skills Exercises Answer Key

page 153
1. Sally Ride
2. George Washington
3. Abraham Lincoln
4. Betsy Ross
5. Martin Luther King, Jr.

pages 154–155
See that student has drawn a line from each child to the correct continent.

pages 156–157
Answers on addresses will vary. See that student has identified correct address for himself or herself.

page 158
1. grass hut on stilts in rain
2. house in snow
3. desert tent
4. house with moderate climate

page 159
1. B, 2
2. A, 4
3. B, 3
4. garden—green
5. C, 4
6. A, 3
7. A, 1
8. clubhouse—red

page 160
See that student has colored flags according to given colors.

page 161
See that trail the student has drawn goes from: Jeff's apartment— Sam's house— south on Maple— swimming pool— slide— back of school— Layla's tree— Maria's yard— sandbox—flagpole.

page 162
See that student has written correct direction in each space, and that pictures are drawn correctly—sun in the east, sunset in the west.

page 163
1. 2012
2. 3
3. 2013
4. 2011
5. 2014
6. 2015

page 164
1. He crossed the river 3 times.
2–7. See that student has drawn and colored according to instructions.

page 165
Down
1. mountain
2. bay
3. globe

Across
4. volcano
5. ocean
6. trees
7. island

page 166
Check to see that the student has colored the map and that Noah's house is colored red.

page 167
Map 3 should be colored.

page 168
Check to see that the student has drawn the lines to the correct words.

page 169
1. Fish Lake Campground
2. Country Shopping Center
3. Berry Town Airport
Map 2

page 170
1. fire station
2. school
3. playground
4. town
5. campground
6. picnic area
7. hospital
8. trees
9. railroad

page 171
Symbols will vary. Check to see that all symbols have been drawn.

page 172
Check that the student has followed directions correctly.

page 173
Check that the student has drawn the path correctly.

page 174
1. Jay
2. Robin
3. Sparrow
4. Blackbird
5. Canary

page 175
Check that the student has drawn the paths correctly.

page 176
Answers will vary according to the size of the thumb! Answers will be approximate.

page 177
1. yes
2. 2
3. 3
4. 2
5. 4
6. 3

page 178
1–4. Check for correct placement on the grid.
5. B, 5
6. D, 2
7. A, 3
8. D, 4

page 179
Check for correct placement on the grid.

pages 180–181
1. planet Earth
2. North America
3. USA
4. Wisconsin
5. Drawings will vary.

pages 182–183
1–7. Check to see that continents are correctly colored.
8. 3
9. no
10. Australia

page 184
Check to see that student has drawn a correct route.

page 185
Check to see that the path is correct and that Benjy's desk is identified.

page 189
Check to see that students have completed drawings to adequately picture the life characteristics.

page 190
Living things are—girl, cat, ducks, rat, butterfly, trees, flowers, bushes, grass, mushrooms, flies, cattails

page 191
Things that are not alive are—houses, driveways, bus, balloon, kite, signs, swings, teeter-totter, bench, drinking fountain, stones, buildings, roads, car, skates, pond, toy boat

page 192
Check to see that leaves are light green, stems are dark green, roots are brown, and flowers are other colors.

page 193
1. seeds germinating
2. little plant
3. bud
4. open flower
5. dandelion fluff
6. seeds blowing
7. plant dies
Numbering of pictures on page is
5—3—2—4—1—6— 7

page 194
Color 2, 3, 4, 5, 6, 7, 8

page 195
Insects with 6 legs—
 1, 2, 3, 4, 6, 7, 8, 9, 10, 12
Spiders with 8 legs—5, 11

page 196
Bird moves from Reptile Cage to Bird Land

Skills Exercises Answer Key

Fish moves from Bird
    Land to Fish Tank
Cat moves from Fish
    Tank to Mammal Land
Ostrich moves from
    Mammal Land to Bird
    Land
Snake moves from
    Mammal Land to
    Reptile Cage

page 197
1. fish—circle in green
2. snail—circle in red
3. frog—circle in yellow
4. ostrich—color
5. bear—circle in blue
6. girl—circle in purple

page 198
1. swim   4. hop
2. fly   5. run
3. climb   6. crawl

page 199
1. dog
2. duck
3. chicken
4. goat
5. rat
6. horse
7. girl

page 200
1. hide
2. make noise
3. sting
4. warn
5. run away

page 201
crocodile to swamp
penguin to iceberg dog
to doghouse fish to fish
bowl bird to tree
Worm is in the right
home—should be
colored.

pages 202–203
pond: frog
desert: lizard
forest: squirrel
rain forest: parrot
grassland: elephant, lion
ocean: octopus
arctic: polar bear

page 204
1. see
2. taste
3. hear
4. smell
5. feel

page 205
Answers may vary some.
1. see, taste, touch
2. see, hear, touch
3. see, hear
4. see, touch
5. hear
6. touch, see
7. Answers will vary.
8. Answers will vary.

page 206
Healthy foods: broccoli,
cherries, oatmeal, fish,
bread, carrots, melon,
celery, oranges, eggplant,
grapes, eggs, milk, cheese

page 207
1. Eat
2. sleep
3. clean
4. day
5. water
6. teeth

page 208
Color: rest, brush teeth,
exercise, check-up, good
food
There are 5 unhealthy
   things.

page 209
Put X on: growling dog,
matches, sharp scissors
There are 7 healthy things.

page 210
Examine chart to see that
the pictures show things
appropriate to the season.

page 211
Check to see that students
have colored the four
ther-mometers with the
correct temperatures.

page 212
There may be some
variation in answers.
1. gas (possibly solid, also)
2. solid
3. solid, gas
4. liquid
5. solid
6. liquid

page 213
Answers may vary. Discuss
these with students. liquids:
water, shampoo, cola
solids: comb, sponge,

hose, can, bone, powder,
collar, brush, clothes, dog,
bubbles, bathtub, Tom,
towel

page 214
1. boil   5. expand
2. bake   6. freeze
3. mix   7. melt
4. burn

page 215
Answers will vary.

page 216
1. A   4. M
2. D   5. Q
3. G

page 217
1. yes   5. no
2. yes   6. no
3. yes   7. yes
4. yes

page 218
X on car, cigarette, spray
can, smokestack

page 219
Check to see that
student's answers are
correct.

page 220
location of arrows:
ball kicker—foot rocket—
back end of rocket
swing—arms pushing
weight lifter—arms lifting
and/or legs sled—arms
pulling Circle the big dog.

page 221
1. no   5. no
2. no   6. yes
3. yes   7. yes
4. no   8. no

page 222
Pictures that should be
found and outlined in red:
   lamp
   lightbulb toaster
   computer
   TV
   vacuum cleaner
Pictures that should be
found and outlined in blue:
   toothbrush
   glasses
   ball
   shoe
6 things use electricity

page 230
50 marbles

page 231
1. 2   4. 10
2. 3   5. 4
3. 5   6. 7

page 232
20 steps

page 233
See that students have
filled in missing numbers
correctly.

page 234
Draw lines from 2 to 56
to make jump ropes.
Students count to 56.

page 235
Fill in the missing
numbers to count 5, 10,
15, 20, 25, 30, 35, 40, 45,
50.
The highest number is
50.
The 2 players making
high five are 25 and 30.

page 236
Missing numbers are
20, 30, 50, 70, 80, 100.

page 237
Look to see that
students have
connected the correct
turtles to ribbons,
colored the ribbons
correctly, and colored
the winning turtle
green.

page 238
21 tiny fish at top—red
19 long-nosed fish on
left— purple
7 large-mouthed fish in
center—orange
11 fat fish to right—
yellow

page 239
Students should add to
the sets:
1 football
1 baseball cap
1 hockey stick
4 hockey pucks
3 golf balls
2 baseball bats

page 240

1. 40
2. 55
3. 75

Bottom—answers should all be "no."

page 241

1. 3   5. 6
2. 9   6. 1
3. 5   7. 10
4. 2

page 242

Look for:
goggles on frog,
yellow duck,
teeth on shark,
turtle's head,
hat on octopus,
and brown dog.

page 243

The team has more than 11 players.

1. 15   7. 90
2. 12   8. 62
3. 71   9. 17
4. 33   10. 8
5. 13   11. 50
6. 51   12. 26

page 244

Numbers should be placed on the fish in accordance with their size.

The largest fish has 6,000 on it and should be colored orange.

page 245

1. 80 + 9
2. 90 + 6
3. 100 + 30 + 3
4. 70 + 5
5. 60 + 9
6. 90 + 8

page 246

Across	Down
A. 23	A. 20
C. 100	B. 30
D. 87	C. 17
E. 65	D. 85
F. 92	E. 66
G. 41	F. 91
H. 60	G. 40

page 247

Hidden clues are the bowling ball and pins. Sport is bowling.

page 248

Left to right, student should draw on dancers:
1. green hoop
2. orange hoop
3. blue hoop
   purple hoop
   yellow hoop
4. red hoop

page 249

1. 5
2. 4
3. 3
4. 10
5. penguins
6. bears
7. snowboards

page 250

The monkey is surfing on a wave in the ocean.

page 251

Answers will vary.

page 252

See that students have drawn lines between the matching words and numbers. There are 10 table tennis balls.

page 253

Answers will vary on estimates. There are 10 mice.

pages 254–255

penny—1¢
nickel—5¢
dime—10¢
quarter—25¢
1. 10¢
2. 30¢
3. 90¢
4. $1.00   Total $2.30

page 256

Check to see that students have drawn toppings in correct fractional sizes.

page 257

The paths students draw may vary, but must connect the following items:

Mike and Mac—
red line joining:
• "one quarter"

• pictured $\frac{1}{4}$ of square
• pictured $\frac{1}{4}$ of circle
• coin—quarter
• $\frac{1}{4}$ fraction written
• "one fourth"
• time—15 minutes

Millie and Mary—
blue line joining:
• "one half"
• pictured $\frac{1}{2}$ of square
• pictured $\frac{1}{2}$ of circle
• coin—half dollar
• $\frac{1}{2}$ fraction written
• time—30 minutes

page 258

1. box around $\frac{1}{2}$
2. circle around $\frac{1}{8}$
3. Answers will vary.
4. Answers will vary.

page 259

See that student has numbered clock correctly.
1. 12
2. 1
3. 1:00
4. 1:30

page 260

1. 5:00
2. 8:00
3. 10:30
4. 12:30
5. 3:00
6. 8:30

page 261

1. clock should show 3:30
2. clock should show 5:00
3. clock should show 6:30
4. clock should show 7:30

page 262

See that students have accurately filled in all dates on the calendar.
1. 3, 10, 17, 24
2. 4
3. 7
4. no
5. Check drawing.

page 263

1. $\frac{1}{2}$ inch
2. $1\frac{1}{2}$ inches

3. 2 inches
4. 1 inch
5. 5 inches
6. $1\frac{1}{2}$ inches
7. 1 inch
8. 2 inches
9. $1\frac{1}{2}$ inches
10. $2\frac{1}{2}$ inches

page 264

1. ounces
2. pounds
3. pounds
4. ounces
5. ounces
6. pounds
7. ounces
8. ounces

page 265

True sentences are 3 and 4.

page 268

1. 7
2. 10
3. 12
4. 13

page 269

1. 2
2. 4
3. 4
4. 1
5. 1
6. 4
7. 1
8. 0

page 270

1. 10
2. 1
3. 9
4. 9 + 10 + 1 = 20

page 271

Missing Numbers on Chart
Elvis....................1
Dino....................7
Dinah.................3
Danny 12
Sally 12
Emma................5
Rico 10
1. 12
2. 5
3. 7
4. 12
5. 10
6. Elvis

Skills Exercises Answer Key

page 272

1. 12
2. 11
3. 12
4. 9
5. 9
6. 8
7. 9
8. 10
9. 11
10. 12
11. 11
12. 12
13. 8
14. 8
15. 11

8 is the lost red boot.

page 273

1. 8
2. 10
3. 11
4. 11
5. 11
6. 6
7. 9
8. 6
9. 9
10. 8
11. 8
12. 7
13. 9
14. 6
15. 5
16. 9

Lulu threw 7 mud pies, and Larry threw 9 mud pies.
Larry threw the most.
Missing numbers are:
1. 4
2. 9

page 274

1. 18
2. 18
3. 17
4. 14
5. 16
6. 18
7. 15
8. 14
9. 17
10. 14
11. 16
12. 15
13. 17
14. 17
15. 16

page 275

Across
A. 19
B. 16
C. 18
D. 20
E. 13
F. 17
G. 14
H. 12

Down
A. 16
C. 10
E. 15
F. 14
G. 11
H. 10

page 276

1. 3
2. 9
3. 19
4. 4
5. 7
6. 13
7. 14
8. 6
9. 1
10. 8
11. 7
12. 9
13. 8
14. 2
15. 5
16. 18
17. 9
18. 0

page 277

Missing numbers are:
1. 4
2. 9
3. 5
4. 6
5. 7
6. 8

page 278

1. 16
2. 17
3. 7
4. 13
5. 7
6. 5
7. 7
8. 16
9. 8
10. 15
11. 14
12. 1
13. 7

14. 5
15. 6

page 279

1. 4 + 5 = 9
2. 5 + 6 = 11
3. 4 + 6 = 10
4. 6 – 3 = 3
5. 3 + 4 = 7
6. 5 – 3 = 2

page 280

1. 7 + 3 = 10
2. 3 + 2 = 5
3. 2 + 1 = 3
4. 5 + 5 = 10
5. 4 –1 = 3

page 281

1. 4
2. 2
3. 7
4. 5
5. 10
6. 0
7. 1
8. 6

page 282

1. 6
2. 5
3. 7
4. 10
5. 10
6. 17
7. 6

page 283

1. 1
2. 10
3. 100
4. 9
5. 99
6. 999
7. 1,000
8. 1,000
9. 0
10. 0
11. 0
12. 0

page 284

Stu	9
Sly	10
Skip	10
Sis	13
Sy	10
Sal	14
Sid	12
Sherm	13
Sue	12

The winner is Sal.

page 285

The ice sculpture will be a skate.
See that all spaces within skate are colored yellow.

1. 8
2. 9
3. 11
4. 16
5. 6
6. 9
7. 23
8. 7
9. 11
10. 8
11. 8
12. 16
13. 19
14. 14
15. 18
16 15
17. 14

page 286

A. –
B. +
C. +
D. +
E. +
F. –
G. –
H. –
I. –
J. +
K. –

page 287

1. 19
2. 27
3. 88
4. 96
5. 39
6. 49
7. 96
8. 66

page 288

1. 79
2. 29
3. 66
4. 28
5. 85
6. 73
7. 38
8. 41
9. 66
10. 38
11. 23

The name of the team is The Frog Legs.

Skills Exercises Answer Key

page 289
1. 73
2. 64
3. 97
4. 28
5. 68
6. 99
7. 57
8. 72
9. 59
10. 68
11. 57
12. 44
13. 59
14. 98
15. 60

page 290
1. 13
2. 15
3. 16
4. 16
5. 14
6. 16
7. 13
8. 14
9. 15
10. 16
11. 13
Tut smashed the most balls.
Check to see that student has colored Tut.

page 291
1. 8
2. 11
3. 8
4. 34
5. 30
6. 57
7. 26
8. 8
9. 60
10. 8
11. 26
12. 33
13. 29
14. 92
15. 11
16. 18
There are 4 eights.

page 292
1. 22
2. 13
3. 47
4. 26
5. 45
6. 33
7. 17
8. 37
9. 65
10. 68
Bottom answers will vary.

page 293
Answers will vary.

page 294
1. 10
2. 40
3. 40
4. 10
5. 20
6. 30
7. 30
8. 20
9. 10
10. 20
11. 30
12. 40
Team colors are:
Team 1—yellow & green
Team 2—orange & blue
Team 3—yellow, green, orange, & blue

page 295
Hank   15¢
Haley   5¢
Hattie   13¢
Hal   14¢
Harry   30¢

pages 296–297
1. 50¢
2. 20¢
3. Moe's eyes
4. 55¢
5. 35¢
6. <
7. <
8. >
9. <
10. <

page 298
Answers will vary.
Check to see that student has added coins accurately.

page 299
1–3. Check to see that student has drawn dots in correct spots.
4. Whale—blue
5. Flamingo—pink

page 300
Check to see that student has drawn hands on the clocks accurately.
1. 2 $\frac{1}{2}$ hours
2. 3 hours

page 301
Alex: 12 o'clock,
        1 o'clock,
        2 o'clock
Amy: 5 o'clock,
       6 o'clock,
       7 o'clock
No.

pages 302–303
1. 5
2. 3
3–4. Check to see that student followed directions correctly.
5. September 5
6. Friday
7. Tuesday
8. September 17

page 304
1. 4
2. 8
3. 6
4. 5
5. rainy
6. sunny

page 305
Circle winners:
Game 1 .... Peanut
Game 2 .... Flash
Game 3 .... Thunder
Game 4 .... Peanut
Game 5 .... Smoky
Game 6 .... Lightning

1. 11
2. 1
3. 0
4. yes

page 306
1. 2nd & 3rd
2. 1st
3. 4th
4. 3rd & 4th
5. Mashers

page 307
1. picnic table
2. drinking fountain
3. teeter-totter
4. sandbox
5. restrooms

page 308
1. 2 + 4 = 6
2. 5 + 6 = 11
3. 2 + 4 + 5 + 6 = 17
   or 6 + 11 = 17
4. 27 − 5 = 22

page 309
1. 1 + 1 = 2
2. 1 + 2 = 3
3. 1 + 2 = 3
4. 2 + 1 + 1 = 4
5. 1 + 1 = 2

page 310
1. 5 − 1 = 4 riders
2. 4 + 2 = 6 days
3. 2 + 1 = 3 hours
4. 2 + 1 + 3 = 6 trips

page 311
Problems will vary.

page 312
Scores will vary.
Score would be 10.
Explanations will vary.

page 313
Cricket jumps the highest.
Explanations will vary.

Skills Exercises Answer Key